Cooking for a
HEALTHY HEART

Cooking for a
HEALTHY HEART

Jacqui Lynas

Bounty Books

Heart UK is an organization for families who have Familial Hypercholesterolaemia (FH) and other inherited forms of hyperlipidaemia. FH is the most common disorder, affecting 1 in 500 of the population. It is an inherited genetic disorder of cholesterol metabolism, resulting in high cholesterol levels and the likelihood of early death from heart disease. Heart UK aims to provide support and encouragement for FH families. If affected families can be identified, screened, diagnosed and treated, then unnecessary tragedies can be prevented and lives saved. You can make a positive difference to your own well-being and to the future of Heart UK. Please help by joining the Heart UK. At just £1 a month it is excellent value. You will receive the Family Heart Digest magazine every two months and have access to the members section of the website. The magazine keeps healthcare professionals and the public right up-to-date with heart disease, with a particular focus on cholesterol.

Heart UK, 7 North Road, Maidenhead, Berkshire SL6 1PE
Tel: 01628 628638
Website: www.heartuk.org.uk
Email: ask@heartuk.org.uk

This book is for my Dad who is a 'great cooker!'

First published in Great Britain in 2002 by
Hamlyn a division of Octopus Publishing Group Ltd

New hardback edition printed in 2003 by Bounty Books,
Reprinted 2004, 2005, 2006, 2008, 2009

This paperback edition published in 2011 by Bounty Books,
a division of Octopus Publishing Group Ltd
Endeavour House
189 Shaftesbury Avenue
London WC2H 8JY

www.octopusbooks.co.uk

An Hachette UK Company
www.hachette.co.uk

Copyright © Octopus Publishing Group Ltd 2002

ISBN· 978-0-753720 49-3

A CIP catalogue record for this book is available from the British Library

Printed and bound in China

NOTES
Both metric and imperial measurements are given for the recipes. Use one set of measures only, not a mixture of both.

Ovens should be preheated to the specified temperature. If using a fan-assisted oven, follow the manufacturer's instructions for adjusting the time and temperature. Grills should also be preheated.

A few recipes include nuts and nut derivatives. Anyone with a known nut allergy must avoid these.

Free-range medium eggs should be used unless otherwise stated. The Department of Health advises that eggs should not be consumed raw. It is prudent for more vulnerable people, such as pregnant and nursing mothers, invalids, the elderly, babies and young children, to avoid uncooked or lightly cooked dishes made with eggs.

Meat and poultry should be cooked thoroughly. To test if poultry is cooked, pierce the flesh through the thickest part with a skewer or fork - the juices should run clear, never pink or red.

All the recipes in this book have been analyzed by the author. The analysis refers to each serving, unless otherwise stated.

Contents

Introduction

Heart disease is now established as the number one killer in the world, claiming more than six million people each year. Nearly all deaths from heart disease are as a result of a heart attack or 'myocardial infarction'. About half of all heart attacks are fatal, and in about a third of them death occurs before reaching hospital. In the UK, heart disease will claim a victim every three minutes, and in the USA, every single minute. Many deaths are premature and family, friends and colleagues are all affected by the tragedy. For those who are lucky enough to survive a heart attack, life is never quite the same again. Heart disease has developed into a lethal epidemic and the problem is set to continue as people live longer and have unhealthy lifestyles.

Yet heart disease is potentially avoidable and preventable. If you want to beat heart disease, rethinking your lifestyle can help reduce many of the risk factors of heart disease such as high cholesterol, high blood pressure, diabetes, smoking and being overweight. If you already have heart disease, it is never too late to re-evaluate your lifestyle, and there is overwhelming evidence that changing your eating habits can save your life.

Dietary advice can be all too confusing, given that we are being bombarded by often conflicting messages, but that's because the effect of diet is complex and there is still much to discover. Simply advocating a low-fat diet is no longer adequate, and current interest is focused on the benefits of a broad-based, multi-faceted dietary approach. This book clearly and concisely explains the latest dietary advice from medical and nutritional experts to help you eat for a healthy heart, and its recommendations are based on consensus opinion and sound scientific research.

How Your Heart Works

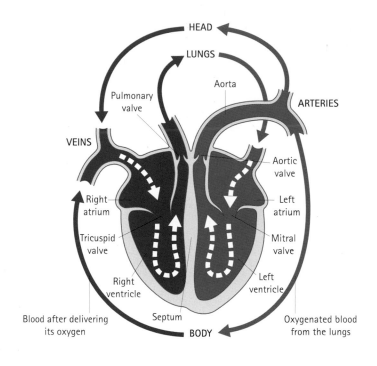

Blood after delivering its oxygen

Oxygenated blood from the lungs

CORONARY ARTERIES AROUND THE HEART

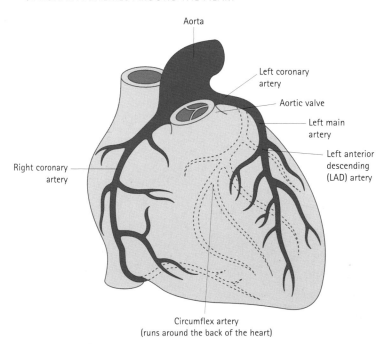

A Strong, Efficient Heart for a Long and Healthy Life

The heart is the powerhouse of the body – the engine that drives blood to all the organs in your body. It is a massively strong muscle, weighing about 340 g or three-quarters of a pound, and is about the size of a clenched fist. It beats tirelessly, 60 to 80 times a minute (and more if you do anything energetic), day and night, automatically pumping out between five and 20 litres (8¾ and 35 pints) of blood every minute, depending on your body's needs. From a baby's conception to the end of its life the heart could beat three billion times!

We feel each heartbeat or contraction of the heart muscle as the pulse. The medical term for this contraction is systole. Diastole describes the relaxation of the heart between beats. The heart has two pairs of chambers, two on the right and two on the left. The right half of the heart pumps blood through the lungs to pick up oxygen, and the left half of the heart pumps oxygen-rich blood, returning from the lungs, to the rest of the body. Every organ in the body needs oxygen to function normally and efficiently. The heart pumps fresh blood through the arteries, thereby delivering oxygen and energy to your body tissues. Carbon dioxide and unwanted waste products are removed from the body tissues via the veins.

Coronary Arteries

To do all this work, the heart muscle itself needs fuel and oxygen for energy, and it gets this from its own blood supply. The blood vessels that supply the heart are called coronary arteries. They need to be tough to cope with the pressure of the beating heart. There are three important coronary arteries. The left coronary artery divides into two large branches, which serve the front and back of the left side of the heart, and the right coronary artery, which is usually one big vessel, serves the right side. The coronary arteries arise from the main artery leaving your heart (the aorta), starting just above the aortic valve. The most important coronary artery is the left main stem, which controls both branches of the left coronary artery and, as a result, most of the blood supply to your heart muscle. The coronary arteries are about the size of a drinking straw, but then divide, getting smaller and smaller (rather like the branches and twigs of a tree) as they grow around the outside of the heart, sending shoots inwards.

Blood Pressure

We all need blood pressure to keep blood flowing round our bodies, delivering oxygen and food to our vital organs. When your heart beats, it pumps blood into your arteries and creates pressure, which causes your blood to flow to all parts of your body. If you're healthy, your arteries are muscular and elastic – they stretch when your heart beats blood through them. As the heart beats, your blood pressure rises and falls when your heart relaxes between beats. Your blood pressure changes each minute, especially with changes in posture, exercise, emotion or when you are sleeping.

Two numbers are recorded when measuring your blood pressure. This is written as 116/58 mmHg (millimetres of mercury), for example. The top number (systolic pressure) measures the pressure in your arteries when the heart beats. The bottom number (diastolic pressure) measures the pressure while your heart rests between beats. There is much debate about what constitutes 'normal' blood pressure, but the latest guidelines suggest that it should be less than 140/90 mmHg (see the table above right). If you have heart disease, it should be less than 140/85 mmHg and even lower if you have diabetes or kidney disease. Several readings should be taken over a period of time before making a judgement about whether or not you have high blood pressure.

Physical Fitness

The size of the heart and how efficiently it beats depend upon your physical fitness. Athletes and people who exercise regularly or are generally very active have larger, stronger hearts which are more efficient – that is, they beat more slowly to deliver the same amount of blood as the heart of a less fit person. Your pulse rate tells you how fast your heart is beating, and the good news is that you can lower your pulse rate by increasing your exercise levels. The latest recommendations for physical activity advise brisk walking for 30 minutes on most days of the week.

Systolic Blood Pressure (mmHg)	
Optimal	120
Normal	130
High normal	130–139

Diastolic Blood Pressure (mmHg)	
Optimal	80
Normal	85
High normal	85–89

ABOVE: Blood pressure is measured with a simple device. A collar is wrapped around the upper arm, then pumped up to make it tight. A dial shows the blood pressure.

What is Heart Disease?

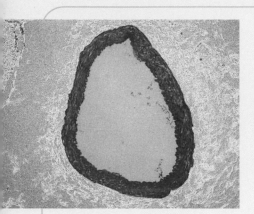

ABOVE: A healthy human coronary artery which is found on the surface of the heart and supplies blood to the heart muscle. The heart muscle is coloured blue in this example. The artery wall is coloured red.

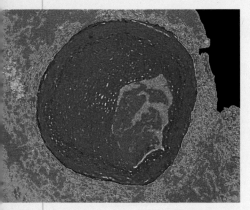

ABOVE: A blocked human artery. The coronary artery (coloured red) lies on the surface of the heart. The narrowed, light brown channel is blocked by a clot and the loss of blood supply to the heart muscle has resulted in a fatal heart attack.

Coronary heart disease (angina and heart attack) occurs when the coronary arteries become narrower or blocked due to ageing, poor diet and an unhealthy lifestyle. Tragically, the process can even begin in childhood. The narrowing of the arteries is due to fatty, cholesterol-laden deposits forming in the smooth artery lining and is called atherosclerosis.

Angina

Narrowed coronary arteries reduce the rate at which blood can be delivered to the beating heart muscle. The muscle doesn't get enough oxygen to fuel the work it is doing and signals this with the pain of angina. Angina is usually felt across the front of the chest but sometimes in the shoulders, arms, throat or jaw. It is usually a heavy or tight pain, generally lasting less than ten minutes. The harder the heart is working, the more oxygen it needs, and therefore angina is usually provoked by exercise and relieved by rest. Angina can also be brought on by strong emotions, eating a heavy meal or going out on a cold day. When angina comes on with increasing severity or frequency, or when it occurs at rest, such as sitting in a chair or lying in bed, the situation is very serious.

Heart Attack

A heart attack occurs when a coronary artery becomes entirely blocked due to the combination of atherosclerosis and the sudden development of a blood clot. The sudden blockage of the artery means that the part of the heart muscle that was supplied by that coronary artery is at once deprived of blood and oxygen. Muscle can't survive without blood, so the affected area of the heart muscle dies and the pain lasts longer than with angina. If only a small area is involved, you have a good chance of recovery. If more muscle is affected, it can cause sudden death in some cases and incomplete recovery since the heart has lost pumping power. Sometimes a heart attack is followed by an abnormal rhythm in the heartbeat (arrhythmia), or a cardiac arrest, when the heart stops altogether.

Cholesterol

Cholesterol, a white waxy substance, is vital for the human body since it forms cell membranes, various hormones, bile salts and vitamin D. However, an excess of cholesterol in the blood can increase your risk of heart disease. A number of factors affect your blood cholesterol levels. Most cholesterol is made in the liver, but some is absorbed from food by the digestive system. Foods high in saturated fat, such as fatty meats and meat products, eggs, butter, cheese, whole milk, cream, pastries, cakes and confectionery, increase your blood cholesterol levels.

'GOOD' AND 'BAD' CHOLESTEROL

Cholesterol travels to your body's cells through the bloodstream in tiny packages called lipoproteins. Scientists distinguish the types of cholesterol packages by their density, and the most important types are low-density lipoprotein cholesterol (LDL cholesterol) and high-density lipoprotein cholesterol (HDL cholesterol). Most of the blood cholesterol is carried as LDL cholesterol from the liver to other parts of the body.

Having a high level of LDL cholesterol increases your risk of heart disease because when oxidized it can slowly build up in the walls of coronary arteries and ultimately cause a heart attack. Therefore, LDL cholesterol can be regarded as the 'bad guy', and the lower the LDL cholesterol level, the better. Your target level of LDL cholesterol should be below 3.0 mmol/l (195 md/dl).

Oxidized LDL cholesterol is taken up by modified white blood cells called macrophages. In time, the macrophages are themselves poisoned by oxidized LDL cholesterol and form moribund 'foam cells' full of cholesterol droplets. Eventually the foam cells die and their toxic contents form, initially the cholesterol deposits of the fatty streaks and later the mature atherosclerotic plaques, which can all lead to damage to the arteries.

ABOVE: Fruit and vegetables rich in antioxidant nutrients protect LDL cholesterol from oxidation. Oxidized LDL cholesterol is toxic, damaging and dangerous, so defend your arteries by eating a wide variety of fruit and vegetables.

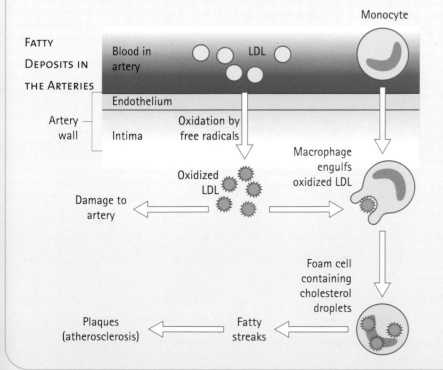

FATTY DEPOSITS IN THE ARTERIES

Monocyte

Blood in artery — LDL

Endothelium

Artery wall — Intima

Oxidation by free radicals

Oxidized LDL

Macrophage engulfs oxidized LDL

Damage to artery

Foam cell containing cholesterol droplets

Plaques (atherosclerosis) ← Fatty streaks

Assessing and Reducing Risk Factors

There are a number of factors that influence the incidence of heart disease.

Factors That Can Be Reduced or Eliminated

High blood cholesterol levels

High blood pressure

Smoking

Diabetes

Being overweight

Lack of physical activity

Factors That You Cannot Change

❤ Age – the older you are, the greater the risk

❤ Gender – women before the menopause are at lower risk of heart disease than men

❤ Family history – you are at increased risk if there is heart disease in your family, especially in a close relative under 55

HDL cholesterol is the 'good guy'. It acts as an arterial scavenger, carrying cholesterol away from body tissues, including artery walls, back to the liver. The higher the HDL cholesterol level, the lower your risk of heart disease. Your target level of HDL cholesterol should above 0.9 mmol/l (35 mg/dl). Experts believe that HDL removes excess cholesterol from atherosclerotic plaques, slowing their build-up.

GETTING TO KNOW YOUR LIPID PATTERN

The fats in your blood are technically known as lipids. If you have a fasting lipid test, where you fast for 12 to 16 hours, drinking only water, the results will reveal your lipid pattern or profile, and this includes total cholesterol, LDL cholesterol, HDL cholesterol and triglyceride levels. A non-fasting lipid test will just measure your cholesterol.

The average cholesterol level of most people in the western world is 5.9 mmols/l (225 mg/dl), yet in areas of rural China the average cholesterol level is 3.0 mmol/l and the rate of heart disease is very low. It is likely that the lower the cholesterol level, the more you reduce your risk of heart disease. If you can keep your total cholesterol level below 5.0 mmol/l (195 mg/dl) for two years, there is a good chance that any atheroma (cholesterol and fatty material) that has already been deposited in your arteries might stabilize or even regress. If you already have heart disease or are at a high risk of developing it, your doctor may have prescribed medication to modify your lipid levels. The benefits of these drugs are significant and their effect is further enhanced by a healthy diet.

Triglycerides

Triglycerides are different fats, which are absorbed from food or made in the body. People with high triglyceride levels often have higher total cholesterol, high LDL cholesterol and low HDL cholesterol. Many clinical studies have shown that people with high triglyceride levels have an increased risk of heart disease. Your target level of triglycerides should be below 1.5 mmol/l (57 mg/dl). Diets high in carbohydrates (particularly simple carbohydrates such as sugar) and alcohol, as well as other factors, can raise triglycerides. People who have diabetes, are overweight or have a high alcohol intake are more likely to have high triglyceride levels. Following a healthy heart diet, with particular emphasis on eating oily fish, can help to lower triglycerides.

High Blood Pressure

If your blood pressure is constantly above 140/90 mmHg, you have high blood pressure or hypertension. This adds to the workload of your heart and arteries.

The heart must work harder than normal and this may cause it to enlarge. As you grow older your arteries will harden and become less elastic, and unfortunately high blood pressure speeds up this process. It can be controlled by a combination of healthy eating, physical activity and medication. The Mediterranean diet, avoiding salt, reducing alcohol and keeping slim, have all been shown to reduce blood pressure.

Diabetes

People with diabetes are at high risk of heart disease, stroke and peripheral vascular disease – any abnormal condition that affects the blood vessels outside the heart and lymphatic vessels – effectively atherosclerosis and non-coronary arteries. In fact, more than two out of three people with diabetes die from cardiovascular disease. If you have diabetes you should pay particular attention to the risk factors for heart disease, follow a healthy lifestyle and use appropriate drug therapy.

Smoking

Smoking cigarettes and other tobacco products raises the risk of heart attack and stroke. Smoking also increases the risk of cancer and lung disease. If you smoke, get help to quit! Even passive smoking significantly increases the risk of heart disease.

Physical Activity

Physical activity helps prevent and treat heart disease, stroke, diabetes, obesity and osteoporosis. It also helps control other major heart disease risk factors such as high blood pressure and high blood cholesterol. Medical studies have shown that just getting our bodies moving every day can have long-term health benefits.

ABOVE: Keeping active will lower your risk of heart disease – even gardening and housework count.

The physical activity needs to be regular, of moderate intensity and aerobic. Aerobic exercise is any activity in which the large muscles in the arms or legs are moving rhythmically such as brisk walking, dancing or cycling. Don't forget that gardening and some household chores can also count as aerobic exercise, such as vigorous weeding or cleaning windows. Even taking the stairs more often or parking your car further away from your destination can help increase your activity levels. Try to do at least 30 minutes of these activities on most days, and if you don't have 30 minutes at a time to spare, try to do 15 minutes twice or ten minutes three times a day. Pick activities that are fun, that suit your needs and that you can do all year round. Get moving and enjoy being active!

Heart Disease Facts and Figures

Heart Facts For Women

❤ Heart disease is not a just a disease that affects men. It accounts for one in five deaths in women, as well as one in four deaths in men.

❤ In the UK in 1997, 64,000 women died from heart disease. This is approximately 375 per day – one every four minutes.

❤ In the USA in 1998 there were 226,467 female deaths from CHD (heart disease) – 49.2 per cent of deaths from CHD – as opposed to 233,374 male deaths – 50.8 per cent. Nearly twice as many women in America die of heart disease and stroke as from all forms of cancer, including breast cancer.

❤ In two-thirds of women who die suddenly from CHD there are no previous symptoms of the disease.

❤ CHD kills three times more women than cancer of the breast, ovary and cervix combined.

❤ According to the most recent calculations, if all major forms of CVD were eliminated, life expectancy would rise by almost seven years, while if all forms of cancer were eliminated, the gain would be three years.

Cardiovascular Disease

The statistics are alarming. Cardiovascular Disease (CVD) is now established as the leading cause of death in the world, killing more than six million people each year. The economic burden and human cost of heart disease are at crisis level now, and if current trends are maintained, by 2020 CVD will be responsible for almost 19 million deaths every year.

CVD is a collective term, which includes coronary heart disease (CHD), stroke and all other diseases of the heart and circulation, such as birth defects and rheumatic heart disease. CVD is the number one killer in the United States; more than 2,600 North Americans die of CVD each day, an average of one death every 33 seconds. More than 150,000 North Americans killed by CVD are under the age of 65 and 34 per cent of deaths from CVD occur prematurely (before the age of 75).

The picture is similar in Europe, where heart disease counts for two million deaths each year and 170,000 people in the EU die from CVD before the age of 65. In the UK, CVD is also the main cause of death, accounting for nearly 257,000 deaths in 1998. More than one in three people can expect to die from CVD. About half of all deaths from CVD are from CHD, and about a quarter are from stroke. CHD caused over 135,000 deaths in the UK in 1998. Despite recent improvements, the death rate from CHD in the UK is still among the highest in the world, although recently exceeded by some of the countries of eastern and central Europe, where death rates are rising rapidly. In Australia, Canada, Sweden, Finland and the Netherlands the death rate is falling more rapidly, particularly for women.

Death statistics are, however, only part of the story, since many individuals are living with the symptoms of heart disease. In the UK, it is estimated that one and a half million people have angina and half a million have heart failure.

Heart Disease Around the World

This table illustrates the death rates for total cardiovascular disease (CVD), coronary heart disease (CHD), stroke and also the total deaths in selected countries.

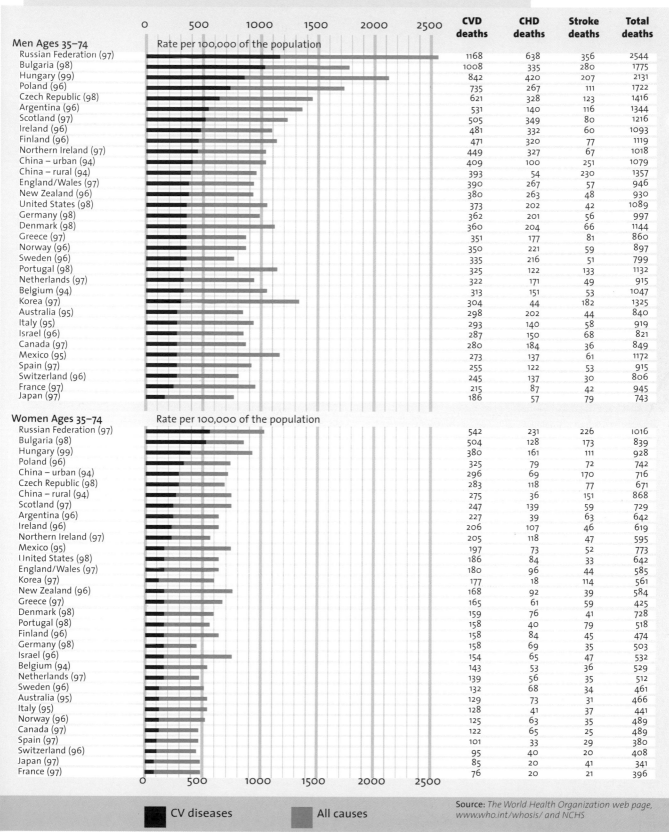

Men Ages 35–74
Rate per 100,000 of the population

Country	CVD deaths	CHD deaths	Stroke deaths	Total deaths
Russian Federation (97)	1168	638	356	2544
Bulgaria (98)	1008	335	280	1775
Hungary (99)	842	420	207	2131
Poland (96)	735	267	111	1722
Czech Republic (98)	621	328	123	1416
Argentina (96)	531	140	116	1344
Scotland (97)	505	349	80	1216
Ireland (96)	481	332	60	1093
Finland (96)	471	320	77	1119
Northern Ireland (97)	449	327	67	1018
China – urban (94)	409	100	251	1079
China – rural (94)	393	54	230	1357
England/Wales (97)	390	267	57	946
New Zealand (96)	380	263	48	930
United States (98)	373	202	42	1089
Germany (98)	362	201	56	997
Denmark (98)	360	204	66	1144
Greece (97)	351	177	81	860
Norway (96)	350	221	59	897
Sweden (96)	335	216	51	799
Portugal (98)	325	122	133	1132
Netherlands (97)	322	171	49	915
Belgium (94)	313	151	53	1047
Korea (97)	304	44	182	1325
Australia (95)	298	202	44	840
Italy (95)	293	140	58	919
Israel (96)	287	150	68	821
Canada (97)	280	184	36	849
Mexico (95)	273	137	61	1172
Spain (97)	255	122	53	915
Switzerland (96)	245	137	30	806
France (97)	215	87	42	945
Japan (97)	186	57	79	743

Women Ages 35–74
Rate per 100,000 of the population

Country	CVD deaths	CHD deaths	Stroke deaths	Total deaths
Russian Federation (97)	542	231	226	1016
Bulgaria (98)	504	128	173	839
Hungary (99)	380	161	111	928
Poland (96)	325	79	72	742
China – urban (94)	296	69	170	716
Czech Republic (98)	283	118	77	671
China – rural (94)	275	36	151	868
Scotland (97)	247	139	59	729
Argentina (96)	227	39	63	642
Ireland (96)	206	107	46	619
Northern Ireland (97)	205	118	47	595
Mexico (95)	197	73	52	773
United States (98)	186	84	33	642
England/Wales (97)	180	96	44	585
Korea (97)	177	18	114	561
New Zealand (96)	168	92	39	584
Greece (97)	165	61	59	425
Denmark (98)	159	76	41	728
Portugal (98)	158	40	79	518
Finland (96)	158	84	45	474
Germany (98)	158	69	35	503
Israel (96)	154	65	47	532
Belgium (94)	143	53	36	529
Netherlands (97)	139	56	35	512
Sweden (96)	132	68	34	461
Australia (95)	129	73	31	466
Italy (95)	128	41	37	441
Norway (96)	125	63	35	489
Canada (97)	122	65	25	489
Spain (97)	101	33	29	380
Switzerland (96)	95	40	20	408
Japan (97)	85	20	41	341
France (97)	76	20	21	396

■ CV diseases ■ All causes

Source: *The World Health Organization web page, www.who.int/whosis/ and NCHS*

The Disease–Diet Link

There is a wealth of information that links diet and the risk of heart disease. The emerging picture is that we should adopt a pattern of eating that can protect against heart disease. But there is no single individual dietary intervention that will guard you against heart disease, and you must look to make several changes to maximize the cardio-protective potential of what you eat.

The classic Seven Countries Study led by Ancel Keys in the 1960s showed a link between saturated fat intake and rate of heart disease in seven different countries. Keys showed that in Japan and the rural Mediterranean countries of southern Europe such as Greece and Italy, where the intake of saturated fat from meat and dairy products was low, there were significantly lower rates of heart disease than in the UK and the USA, where intakes of saturated fat were higher.

ABOVE AND BELOW: Mediterranean lifestyle has long been known to be healthy. We now know that an abundance of fresh fruit, vegetables and olive oil play a significant part.

The case of France, however, is very interesting, since the French have a high total fat intake yet lie low in the international league table for heart disease. There has been much debate about this 'French paradox', and the conclusion drawn is that other mechanisms must be at work.

The Mediterranean Diet

The characteristic Mediterranean diet is high in fruit, vegetables, bread and other forms of cereals, potatoes, beans, nuts and seeds. It features olive oil as an important fat source, while dairy products, fish, poultry and eggs are consumed in low to moderate amounts. Little red meat is eaten, but a glass or two of wine compensates!

A Mediterranean-style diet certainly has a favourable effect on blood cholesterol concentrations. So what are the possible heart-protective mechanisms behind the Mediterranean-style diet?

OLIVE OIL

Olive oil contains mainly monounsaturated fat and when used to replace saturated fat in the diet lowers total and LDL cholesterol without decreasing the 'good guy' HDL cholesterol. Substituting saturated fat with high levels of polyunsaturated fat or carbohydrates can produce the undesirable effect of decreasing HDL cholesterol.

FRUIT AND VEGETABLES

Another significant factor is that the Mediterranean-style diet is high in fruit and vegetables, which are rich in vitamins and minerals, essential fatty acids and antioxidants. There are about 600 antioxidants and these include the ACE vitamins, (beta-carotene, which is converted to vitamin A in the body, vitamin C and vitamin E), minerals (selenium and zinc) and various other compounds that give fruit and vegetables their fabulous colours (flavonoids and phenols). Red wine and tea are also known to be good sources of antioxidants. The antioxidants do exactly what their name implies – they protect LDL cholesterol from becoming oxidized. Oxidized LDL cholesterol is much more toxic than LDL cholesterol and more likely to accumulate in the artery walls. Fruit and vegetables also supply other protective nutrients. For example, folic acid is found in dark green vegetables, fruit and whole grains, and helps to maintain lower levels of homocysteine in the blood. High levels of homocysteine are linked to an increased risk of heart disease.

ABOVE: Berries, such as raspberries and strawberries are full of useful antioxidants which may be essential in maintaining a healthy heart.

THE EVIDENCE

The Lyon Diet Heart Study, carried out in Lyon, France by A. Lorgeril *et al* and first published in 1994, provided evidence that if you have had a heart attack and subsequently adopt a Mediterranean-style diet, you can expect a dramatic reduction on the risk of recurrent heart attacks.

The Benefits of Soya Beans

In Asian countries, with traditionally high intakes of soya-bean products, there is also a lower incidence of cardiovascular disease. Soya beans contain phytoestrogens, naturally occurring compounds that bear a structural similarity to oestrogen. Phytoestrogens have a beneficial effect on the lipid pattern (see page 12), especially in post-menopausal women. In addition, isoflavones in soya products exert a favourable effect on the lining of blood vessels and improve vascular tone.

BELOW: Countries which consume a lot of soya beans also have lower levels of cardiovascular disease due to the phytoestrogens in beans.

The Benefits of Omega-3

One of the most remarkable dietary discoveries in recent years has been the role fish can play in preventing heart disease. People who eat fish and shellfish regularly, such as the Japanese and Greenland Inuits, have fewer heart attacks than non-fish eaters. Oily fish is the richest source of the polyunsaturated fatty acids – eicosapentanoic acid (EPA) and docosahexanoic Acid (DHA), or omega-3 fatty acids.

Results of the DART (Diet and Reinfarction Trial, carried out in Wales by M. L. Burr *et al*, published 1989) gave evidence that if you have had a heart attack, eating two or three portions of oily fish per week could reduce your chances of having another, so fish can save your life as well.

Omega-3 fatty acids are also found in plants. An example is alpha-linolenic acid, found in seed oils, soya, nuts and green vegetables, which can actually make EPA and DHA in the body. Omega-3 fatty acids can play an important part in blood-clotting mechanisms, making the blood less sticky and reducing the risk of thrombosis. They also reduce irregular and potentially fatal heart arrhythmias. The spread used in the Lyon Diet Heart Study was made from rapeseed oil and was rich in alpha-linolenic acid.

Popping Pills Versus Real Food

Recent well-designed clinical trials (MRC/BHF Heart Protection Study, R. Collins, (UK), published 2002; GISSI study, R. Marchioli, (Italy), published 1999) have confirmed that there seems little benefit in taking individual nutrients such as vitamin E, C or beta-carotene in supplement form as vitamin preparations. This would suggest that the benefit may only occur when the antioxidants are taken as part of a healthy eating pattern, containing plenty of whole foods, including fruit and vegetables. However, if you can't eat fish, or don't like it, it is a good idea to take a supplement of omega-3 fatty acids (EPA and DHA) in capsule form, at 1 g per day.

Shaping Up

The shape you are has a link with heart disease. If you are apple-shaped, where fat is deposited around your stomach, you are at greater risk of heart disease than if you are pear-shaped, with fat distributed over your hips and thighs. This is because fat cells over the stomach make the body more resistant to the hormone insulin. To compensate, more insulin is produced, which increases blood pressure, cholesterol and triglycerides, lowers HDL cholesterol and increases the tendency for the blood to form clots. And of course your risk of becoming diabetic is increased. This clustering of risk factors is called the Insulin Resistance Syndrome.

There is now evidence that men and women who keep to foods with a low glycaemic index are less likely to develop insulin resistance, diabetes and heart disease. Glycaemic index (GI) is a measurement of the effects of carbohydrate-rich foods on blood glucose levels. Starchy foods that take a long time to be digested and absorbed into the body have a low GI, and these foods have a favourable effect on blood glucose and insulin. This improves the balance of blood lipids, increasing the protective HDL cholesterol and lowering triglyceride levels.

ABOVE: Eat up your greens! Valuable omega-3's can also be found in plant sources so supplement your oily fish with dark green leafy vegetables, pumpkins, sweet potatoes, seed oils, soya and nuts.

Top Ten Tips for Healthy Living

Tip 1   Enjoy a Wide Variety of Nutritious Foods

Eat a combination of different food, which will help give you all the essential nutrients in balanced proportions. Try to adopt the Mediterranean diet most of the time (see page 16). This should be a lifelong approach, not just a five-minute wonder, so make it easy for yourself by making simple changes one at a time. Don't be too hard on yourself if you sometimes have lapses – just restart and try again. Above all, enjoy your food!

Tip 2   Be a Healthy Weight for Your Height

Make sure you keep to a healthy weight for your height by monitoring your waist measurement. Do you need to lose inches? Measure your waist and find out.

You should aim to keep your waist circumference in the healthy range – less than 93 cm (37 inches) for men and 80 cm (32 inches) for women. If your waist measurement is more than this, try to lose weight and get as close to these figures as possible, but remember that any decrease in your waist measurement is progress. Lose weight by reducing your energy intake to less than your body needs and increase your physical activity at the same time. Be honest with yourself and watch those portion sizes!

Tip 3   Eat Plenty of Fruit, Vegetables and Salad

You should eat at least five portions a day, but what exactly is a portion. See the box opposite for an at-a-glance guide.

An easy tip to remember is that a portion of fruit or vegetables is about the size of a clenched fist and that five portions should add up to 500 g (1 lb) in weight.

Waist Measurements

MEN

93–100 cm (37–40 inches): you are overweight

Over 100 cm (40 inches): you are fat

WOMEN

80–88 cm (32–35 inches): you are overweight

Over 88 cm (35 inches): you are fat

- Measure with a tape measure next to your skin, not over your clothes
- Make sure the tape is level at the navel
- Let the tape fit around your waist – don't pull too tightly
- Try to measure in the same place each time

Portion Guide

- 1 large fruit (such as an apple, orange or banana)
- 2 small fruits (such as plums or satsumas)
- 1 cup of raspberries, strawberries or grapes
- 1 glass (150 ml/¼ pint) of fruit juice
- 1 tablespoon of dried fruit
- 2 tablespoons of raw, cooked or frozen vegetables
- 1 dessert bowl of salad

Tip 4 Eat Fish Two or Three Times a Week

Eat more fish, particularly oily fish, especially if you have already had a heart attack. Oily fish are the richest source of omega-3 fatty acids (EPA and DHA – see pages 17 and 18). EPA and DHA can also be made in the body from alpha-linolenic acid, which is found in plant food sources.

White fish, such as cod, haddock, bass, flatfish, red snapper and dogfish, contain some omega-3 fatty acids, although not enough for them to be classified as oily fish. Shellfish contain small amounts of omega-3. The amount of omega-3 in fish also varies with the seasons, and whether the fish is wild or farmed.

If you can't eat fish, you should take a daily supplement of 1 g of omega-3 fatty acids. Look out for a special variety of eggs that contain omega-3, produced by chickens that have been fed an omega-3-packed diet.

BELOW: Stick to the advice in Tip 4 to ensure that your diet is getting an optimum amount of omega-3 fatty acids. If you do not eat fish, there are plenty of plant sources that will provide sufficient amounts as well.

Top Fish Sources of Omega-3

	(omega-3 per portion)
Mackerel	4.5 g
Pilchards (canned in tomato sauce)	3.2 g
Trout	2.9 g
Salmon	2.5 g
Salmon (canned)	1.9 g
Sardines (canned in tomato sauce)	2.0 g
Herring	2.2 g
Crab (canned)	0.9 g

Top Plant Sources of Omega-3

	(omega-3 per portion)
Flaxseed and flaxseed oil (linseeds and linseed oil)	1.8 g
Walnuts and walnut oil	1.5 g
Rapeseed oil	1.1 g
Soya-bean oil	0.8 g
Sweet potatoes and pumpkins	1.3 g
Spinach and leafy green vegetables	0.2 g

Tip 5   Base Meals and Snacks Around Wholegrain Foods

Wholegrain foods include bread, cereals, rice, pasta and starchy food, such as potatoes. They are filling yet not fattening and are great sources of fibre, both soluble and insoluble. Some starchy foods have a better effect on your body weight, lipid and glucose metabolism than others, and these are foods with a low glycaemic index (GI – see page 18). The GI of a food tells you how fast it causes blood glucose and insulin levels to rise. The lower the GI, the slower the food is digested and absorbed and the better the effect on blood insulin, glucose and lipid levels.

Low GI Foods

New potatoes

Basmati rice

Apples, pears, plums

Pasta

Beans

Oats

 SOURCES OF FIBRE

Soluble – lowers cholesterol

Oats – rolled oats, oat bran, oat-based cereals and breads

Beans – peas, split peas, lentils, chickpeas, soya beans and baked beans

Some fruits – apples, strawberries and citrus fruits

Insoluble – prevents bowel problems

Wholegrain bread and cereals

Brown rice

Wholemeal pasta

Fruit and vegetables

BELOW: If you want to use a spread choose a low fat version made from vegetable oils that will help you to lower your cholesterol.

Tip 6   Eat a Diet Low in Fat, Especially Saturated Fat

There are three main types of fat in food – saturated, monounsaturated and polyunsaturated. All fatty foods are made up from a mixture of these three types but are classified according to the type of fat present in the largest amount. Trans fats are found in certain foods in small amounts and behave much like saturated fats.

SATURATED FATS

Found in: Fatty meats, full-cream dairy products such as milk, cream and cheese, coconut and palm oil used in convenience foods, cakes, pastries, biscuits, sweets, pre-packed foods and take-away meals.

Effect: Raise cholesterol

Best Choice Oils

Saturated fat per   100 g (31/2 oz)

Olive oil	14.0 g
Rapeseed oil	6.6 g

Monounsaturated fat per 100 g

Olive oil	69.7 g
Rapeseed oil	57.2 g

Polyunsaturated fat per 100 g

Olive oil	11.2 g
Rapeseed Oil	31.5 g

❤   TRANS FATS

Found in: Small amounts in the fat of dairy products and some meats but mainly in hydrogenated vegetable oils, some margarines and in commercially prepared foods such as biscuits, pastries, cakes, puddings and baked goods.
Effect: Raise cholesterol

❤   POLYUNSATURATED FATS

Found in: Vegetable oils such as sunflower, corn, safflower, soya, grapeseed and nut oils and many margarines and spreads contain omega-6 polyunsaturated fatty acids Vegetables and fish oils contain omega-3 fatty acids.
Effect: Lower cholesterol
Lower tendency of blood to clot
Lower triglyceride levels
Protect heart from arrhythmias (irregular heartbeats)

❤   MONOUNSATURATED FATS

Found in: Olive and rapeseed (canola) oil, peanut oil and spreads, avocados and nuts.
Effect: Lower cholesterol

You should avoid saturated fat and choose fats that are unsaturated, particularly olive oil and rapeseed (canola) oil. Rapeseed oil is a good source of omega-3 fatty acids and is increasingly the chosen oil for most unspecified vegetable oils, but always check the label.

New spreads which contain plant sterols are available for people with raised cholesterol. These can achieve a ten to 15 per cent reduction in LDL cholesterol when eaten as part of a healthy diet. Plant sterols, also known as phytosterols, occur naturally in plants. They can be found in vegetable oils such as sunflower, rapeseed and soya bean and in nuts, seeds and grains, and lower cholesterol in the blood by reducing the absorption of cholesterol from the intestine. They are extracted, concentrated and added to various foods such as spreads, soft cheese, yogurt and cereal bars.

How much fat should you eat in a day?

A healthy fat intake is based on your energy needs and activity levels. An average man may require 2500 kcals (calories) per day and an average woman 2000 kcals per day. You need to limit your total fat intake so that around 35 per cent or less of your total calories come from fat.

If you need to lose weight, you should reduce your entire fat intake and this means even the good fats, since all fat is fattening! Use low-fat cooking methods such as microwaving, grilling, griddling, steaming, baking, casseroling and stewing.

Daily Guidelines for Fat Intake

INTAKE IN KILOCALORIES (KILOJOULES)	TOTAL FAT IN GRAMS	SATURATED FAT IN GRAMS
1500 (6270)	57	15
1800 (7524)	68	18
2000 (8360)	70	23
2500 (10450)	95	32

Cooking the Oil-water Spray Way

You can reduce the fat in cooking by using an oil-water spray, which delivers far less oil than commercial oil sprays. Fill a small plastic spray bottle with seven-eighths water and one-eighth oil of your choice.

The following oils are perfect for roasting or grilling:
- ♥ olive
- ♥ rapeseed
- ♥ safflower
- ♥ sunflower

Or, for salads and oriental dishes try using:
- ♥ walnut
- ♥ sesame oil

Use your oil-water spray when cooking under the grill, in a griddle pan, in a frying pan or in roasting pans before adding foods. Alternatively, actually spray the food for grilling, griddling, frying and roasting to give the lightest possible coating of oil. So don't brush – spray!

ABOVE: Experiment with the oil-water spray when griddling – try it on lean pork steaks for example, and accompany with steamed vegetables for an ultra healthy supper.

Tip 7   Choose Lean Meat, Poultry, Eggs, Beans, Nuts, Soya and Low-fat Dairy Foods

Eat a variety of protein foods – choose a different one each day. Pulses are good for your heart: peas, beans (including baked, kidney, soya, borlotti and butter beans), lentils and chickpeas are great sources of soluble fibre, which can help lower cholesterol. Soya protein also has a similar benefit. Nuts protect you from heart disease, since they contain alpha-linolenic acid, folic acid, vitamin E and arginine, so eat a few unsalted nuts every day. You can eat up to four eggs a week and still be within the recommended daily intake of 15–32 g of saturated fat and 300 mg of cholesterol (depending on your calorie intake). Each egg yolk contains 1.5 g of saturated fat and 200 mg of cholesterol.

Tip 8   Avoid Too Much Salt

Three quarters of our salt intake now comes from salt added to processed food. So choose fresh foods rather than processed wherever possible, for example fresh meat and fish, fruit and vegetables.

ABOVE: Salt increases blood pressure so should definitely be kept out of any kitchen that is dedicated to a healthy heart diet.

♥ Avoid obviously salty foods – salted nuts, crisps, canned fish, ham, bacon, sausages, corned beef, canned foods, packet soups, commercial pies, cheeses and salad dressings.

♥ The easiest way to cut your salt intake is not to add it to food, either while cooking or at the table. Rock salt and sea salts are also sodium chloride and should be avoided. Replace the taste with fresh and dried herbs as well as other flavourings such as lemon juice, garlic, ginger and vinegars.

♥ Remember some foods that do not appear to be salty, such as bread and some cereals, do contain large quantities of salt. Again, check the label!

Keep an especially close eye on salt levels if you are using stocks in cooking. The homemade stocks on page 138, as well as being delicious, are fat-free and far lower in salt than stock made with commercial stock cubes. If you have to resort to stock cubes, use half a cube to 300 ml (½ pint) water. The stock will keep in the refrigerator for up to one week and in the freezer for two to three months. You should be aware that a commercially-produced stock cube can provide 1 g of fat , of which negligible is saturated and over 1000 mg of sodium.

Try to keep to the following handy hints:
- ❤ Omit the stock cube if you can
- ❤ If not, use half a stock cube instead of a whole one
- ❤ Look out for lower salt and lower fat stock cubes
- ❤ Better still, make and freeze your own!
- ❤ Use flavoursome vegetables such as onions, garlic, leek, carrots, ginger and canned tomatoes

Tip 9   Enjoy Alcohol With Your Food but be Sensible

If you like alcohol, then enjoy a unit or two each day with your meal. It is the pattern of drinking and the amount you consume that are the important factors rather than the type of drink. Avoid binge drinking and keep to safe levels of alcohol, with some alcohol-free days.

Tip 10   Try to Walk for Half an Hour Most Days

Eating for a healthy heart is part of a whole healthy lifestyle, which involves not smoking and being physically active. Brisk walking, cycling or climbing the stairs will benefit your heart. This will help you get fitter, control your weight and improve your HDL cholesterol. So keep moving!

Units of Alcohol

1 unit of alcohol =
1 small beer, lager or cider
(300 ml/½ pint)
1 small glass of red or white wine
(125 ml/4 fl oz)
1 measure of spirits
(25 ml/1 fl oz)
1 small glass of fortified wine,
e.g. sherry, Martini
(50 ml/2 fl oz)

LEFT: Don't worry if you do not enjoy exercise – try and find something active that you know you will be able to include in your day-to-day life. Even 'just walking' is perfectly suitable.

A Healthy Heart Diet

	Best Choice	In Moderation	Best Avoided
Cereals & Starchy Foods	Bread, chapattis, breakfast cereals, oats, porridge, rice, pasta, popcorn (without butter), all other cereals	Naan bread	Poppadoms (fried), waffles, croissants, Danish pastries, fried rice, noodles in cartons
Potatoes	Boiled, mashed, jacket, instant (without fat)	Oven chips, roast potatoes cooked in best-choice oil, fat-free crisps	Chips, potato croquettes, all other crisps
Vegetables & Fruit	A wide variety of vegetables, fruit, salads, pulses – raw, baked, boiled, steamed, and all fresh, frozen, dried, canned	Stir-fried vegetables in best-choice oils, coleslaw in homemade dressing, canned fruit in syrup	Ready-made coleslaw; vegetables in batter
Fish	White fish: cod, haddock, plaice, lemon sole, whiting; oily fish: mackerel, herring, salmon, tuna and trout; canned fish in water or tomato sauce: tuna, pilchards, sardines; shellfish: oysters, mussels, clams, whelks, winkles, scallops; squid	Canned fish in oil (drain or rinse off excess oil); fish in breadcrumbs; shellfish: shrimps, prawns, lobster, crab	Fried fish in batter: scampi, whitebait; roe, fish pâté, taramasalata
Meat	Well-trimmed grilled steak, chicken and turkey (with skin removed), venison, rabbit	Lean lamb, beef, pork; lean minced beef; grilled lean burgers; lean ham, gammon and lean bacon; liver and kidney; low-fat sausage	Fatty meats, crackling and skin; duck, sausages , sausagemeat, luncheon meat, corned beef, pâté, Scotch eggs, meat pies and pasties
Vegetarian Choices	Mycoprotein (Quorn), tofu, soya protein, pulses, chestnuts	All fresh nuts	Check fat content of vegetarian ready-made dishes

	Best Choice	In Moderation	Best Avoided
Eggs & Dairy 	Egg white, skimmed milk, low-fat yogurt, very low-fat cheese: cottage, fat-free fromage frais	Semi-skimmed, soya, goats', sheep's milk and their products; Greek yogurt, fromage frais, crème fraîche, evaporated milk; cheese: reduced-fat hard cheese, Edam, brie, camembert, feta, ricotta, mozzarella, cheese spread	Whole eggs (no more than four a week); whole milk, condensed milk, cream; cheese: Cheddar, Gouda, Gruyère, Roquefort, Stilton, cream cheese
Oils 	Olive oil, rapeseed oil	Sunflower, corn, safflower, groundnut and sesame seed oils	Lard, suet, ghee and some vegetable oils, particularly palm and coconut oil
Spreads 	Plant sterol or stanol spreads, low-fat spreads	Olive, rapeseed, sunflower and soya oil spreads	Butter, hard margarines
Whole Meals 	Pasta with vegetable sauce, paella, kedgeree, kebabs skewered with best-choice ingredients, homemade soups	Homemade pizza, cottage pie, chilli con carne, fish pie, casseroles	Fish and chips, lasagne, pasta in cream sauce, pies, quiches, samosas, cream soups
Cakes & Biscuits 	Homemade using best-choice ingredients; crispbreads, crumpets, rice cakes, matzos, breadsticks	Currant buns, scones, tea bread, malt loaf, fatless sponge; plain and semi-sweet biscuits, crackers	Cakes: ready-made, rich, sponge, fresh cream; doughnuts, pastries, chocolate biscuits
Puddings 	Homemade using best-choice ingredients; meringue, low-fat milk puddings, jelly, sorbet	Frozen yogurt, ice cream, milk puddings, crumbles	Cheesecake, pastry, suet puddings
Flavourings, Sauces, Jams & Sweets 	Pepper, herbs, spices, lemon juice, vinegar, garlic, tomato purée, mustard; homemade salad dressings and sauces made with best-choice ingredients; jam, marmalade, honey	Tomato ketchup, brown sauce, Worcestershire sauce, pickles, Bovril, Marmite, stock cubes, gravy granules, reduced-calorie mayonnaise and salad cream; hummus, peanut butter; mints and boiled sweets	Salt, salad cream, mayonnaise, cream sauces, ready-made cook-in sauces, chocolate spread, chocolates, toffees, fudge

Making Changes

Do You Eat This?

Breakfasts

Sweetened cereal with milk	Fried egg and bacon
Toast and butter	Croissants with egg and bacon

Main Meals

Fried fish and chips	Fried sausage and chips
Steak and kidney pie or pudding	Stew and dumplings

Desserts

Apple pie and cream	Steamed sponge and custard
Gateau or cheesecake	Individual mousse

Snacks

Sausage roll	Chocolates, sweets, crisps
Pie or pasty	Doughnuts, pastries
Chips	Biscuits
Cheese and biscuits	Cheese sandwich

Try Switching To This

Breakfasts

Unsweetened cereal or porridge with skimmed or semi-skimmed milk and fruit	Grilled lean bacon, poached egg and wholemeal toast
Wholemeal or wholegrain toast and low-fat spread, unsaturated spread, plant stanol or sterol spread	

Main Meals

Baked fish, oven chips and peas	Grilled sausage, jacket potato and baked beans
Cottage pie	Casserole with beans and potato topping

Desserts

Baked apple and low-fat custard	Low-fat milk pudding with dried fruit
Fruit-filled meringue shells	Natural yogurt or fromage frais with fresh fruit

Snacks

Low-fat cheese sandwich with wholemeal bread	Tea breads, teacakes, scones
Lean meat or tuna salad and wholemeal roll	Wholemeal or wholegrain rolls, sandwiches, toast
Lentil soup and wholemeal roll	Fresh fruit, unsweetened breakfast cereals
Jacket potato and baked beans	Vegetable batons, dried fruit

REMEMBER TO EAT A PORTION OF FRUIT, VEGETABLES OR SALAD WITH EVERY MEAL

Check the Label!

To help you make the appropriate choices when buying food, always check the label. A lot of food eaten today is processed and it is sometimes difficult to know exactly what you are eating. Processed food has to have a label listing the main ingredients. The ingredients are always listed in order of weight, so that the main ingredient is first on the list.

Since you won't have time while shopping to read everything, here are some details that you can check at a glance.

Nutritional Information

Check the energy (kcals), fat and saturated fat per 100 g (3½ oz) or per serving. Compare similar products and choose the brand with the lowest figures. The fat content is probably the most useful piece of information.

UNDERSTANDING THE FAT CONTENT

The table opposite will help you to understand the details of fat content on food labels. In the example given here, the pizza contains nearly 20 g of fat and therefore one-third to one-fifth of the recommended fat for a day.

CHECKING PORTION SIZES

For meals and foods that you eat in large quantities, look at the amount per serving. For snacks and foods that you eat in small amounts, look at the 'per 100 g' information. Work out from the 'Ready reckoner' below whether there is a little or a lot of each nutrient in the food. Remember that the most important items to look for are calories, fat and sodium (salt).

CALCULATING THE SALT CONTENT

If you want to know the amount of salt (sodium chloride) in a product, multiply the sodium by 2.5 (1 g of sodium per 100 g (3½ oz) = 2.5 g salt per 100 g (3½ oz)). Try to keep your daily sodium intake to below 2.5 g = 2500 mg sodium = 6 g salt. In practice, this is hard to do since most of our daily intake comes from processed foods.

As a general rule, reject any food that has more than 5 g fat per 100 g (3½ oz), especially when most of the fat is in the form of saturates. Choose oils and spreads that are rich in monounsaturates, and remember to avoid hydrogenated vegetable oil (trans fats).

Label Checklist

Choose foods making general claims such as:

- ❤ Healthy eating
- ❤ Diet, reduced-calorie or low-calorie
- ❤ Reduced-fat, low-fat or virtually fat-free
- ❤ Sugar-free
- ❤ Low-salt or reduced-salt

But beware:

- ❤ Some low-fat products may be full of sugar and therefore higher in calories than the standard product
- ❤ Cholesterol-free foods may still have plenty of fat and calories
- ❤ Sugar-free doesn't mean low-calorie or low-fat; such foods may be high in both

Reading Labels

The example below shows you how to read a food label and get the information you need. Use it in conjunction with the nutritional information opposite and the Ready Reckoner below to make sure you know exactly what you are eating.

energy • measured in calories (kcal)
- the amount of energy that a food gives you
- the Guideline Daily Amounts is 2500 kcal (10450 Kj) for men and 2000 kcal (8360 Kj) for women

protein • measured in grams (g)
- most people eat more than enough protein so special guidelines aren't needed

carbohydrate • measured in grams (g)
- this includes sugars and starches
- it includes natural and added sugars
- **'of which sugars'** this is the amount of carbohydrate that comes from sugar

fat • measured in grams (g)
- the total amount of fat in the food
- includes saturates, polyunsaturates and monounsaturates
- eat less of all types especially saturates
- the Guideline Daily Amounts (GDA) is 95 g for men and 70 g for women

fibre • measured in grams (g)
- fibre is found in veggies, fruit, beans and pulses
- the Guideline Daily Amounts (GDA) is 18 g for adults

sodium • measured in grams (g)
The Guideline Daily Amounts (GDA) is 2.5 g for adults

Tomato and Mozzarella Pizza

INGREDIENTS

Wheat flour, tomato (17%), water, mozzarella cheese (13%), olive oil, vegetable oil, yeast, oregano

NUTRITIONAL INFORMATION (typical values)

PER 100g AS CONSUMED		PER 150g (HALF PIZZA)
energy	229 kcals	344 kcal
	966 Kj	1445 Kj
protein	8.8 g	13.2 g
carbohydrate	33.6 g	50.4 g
fat	6.6 g	9.9 g
(of which saturates)	2.8 g	4.2 g
(monounsaturates)	2.6 g	4.0 g
(polyunsaturates)	1.2 g	1.7 g
fibre	2.0 g	3.0 g
sodium	2.7 g	4.1 g

'Ready Reckoner' Guide to Food Labelling (figures per 100 g/3½ oz)

A lot		A little	
	10 g of sugars		2 g of sugars
	20 g of fat		3 g of fat
	5 g saturated fat		1 g of saturated fat
	3 g of fibre		0.5 g of fibre
	500 mg sodium		100 mg of sodium

Source: The British Heart Foundation

Menu Planner

Eating as a Family

Lean Lasagne (see pages 92–3)

Potato and Olive Bread (see pages 86–7)

Mediterranean Vegetable and Walnut Salad with Olive Vinaigrette page (see page 56)

Mango and Pineapple Pavlova (see pages 132–3)

Vegetarian Dinner

Vegetarian Cider & Sage Sausages (see page 104)

Garlic Mash (see page 88)

Caponata Ratatouille (see page 64)

Lemon Ricotta Cheesecake with Blueberries (see pages 130–1)

Summer Weekend Party

Garlic, Pea and Parmesan Crostini (see pages 54–5)

Griddled Honey-Glazed Tuna with Parsnip Purée (see pages 87–90)

Baked Beetroot, Spinach & Orange Salad (see pages 60–1) with a green leafy salad

Summer Pudding with fromage frais (see page 131)

Winter Supper Party

Fennel and White Bean Soup (see pages 52–3) with fresh wholegrain rolls

Cranberry and Orange Turkey Fillets (see page 119)

Spiced Roast Roots (see page 70) with green leafy vegetables

Apple and Fig Crumble pages (see pages 128–9)

Quick Menu

Thai Beef and Mixed Pepper Stir-Fry (see page 118) with noodles

Crisp green salad

Platter of fresh fruit

Children's Choice

Roasted Red Pepper and Spring Onion Dip with Vegetable Batons (see pages 46–7)

Tomato and Herb Pizza Pie (see page 103)

Mixed Salad with Fruity Dressing (see page 139)

Banana and Raisin Teabread (see page 136)

recipes

This section presents more than 80 easy-to-follow, delicious recipes using a variety of foods and cooking styles. Some recipes feature more unusual ingredients and fresh flavours to stimulate your taste buds, while others are healthy, heart-promoting versions of traditional, familiar and comforting dishes. Whichever you choose, not only will you be taking the best care of your heart but ensuring your wellbeing as a whole.

Use this at a glance guide to the Top Ten Tips for a Healthy Heart Diet (see pages 19–25 for a more detailed explanation) as a starter to planning your meals from this recipe section.

1. Enjoy a wide variety of nutritious foods.

2. Be a healthy weight for your height.

3. Eat plenty of fruit, vegetables and salad.

4. Eat fish two or three times a week.

5. Base your meals and snacks around plenty of wholegrain foods.

6. Eat a diet low in fat, particularly saturated fat.

7. Choose lean meat, poultry, eggs, beans, nuts, soya and low-fat dairy foods.

8. Eliminate salt from your diet or keep it to a minumum wherever possible.

9. Enjoy alcohol with your food but keep to sensible limits.

10. Keep active.

walnut & banana sunrise smoothie

Preparation time: 10 minutes   **Serves 2**

1 Place all the ingredients in a food processor or blender and blend until smooth and frothy. Pour into 2 glasses.

OR YOU COULD TRY...

Choose your own mixture of delicious fresh fruits, prepare as necessary, then whiz them up with nothing more than a handful of crushed ice. Try a mixture of the following:

1 banana, 2 handfuls fresh or frozen blackberries, 1 handful chopped fresh pineapple, 150 ml (5 oz) natural yogurt, 150 ml (¼ pint) skimmed milk; or 2 handfuls fresh strawberries, 1 handful raspberries, 150 g (5 oz) strawberry soya yogurt, 150 ml (¼ pint) soya milk

1 orange, segmented

1 banana

150 ml (¼ pint) skimmed milk

150 g (5 oz) natural yogurt

25 g (1 oz) walnuts

3 teaspoons honey

NUTRITIONAL FACTS   ⊙ Kcals – 300 (1254 Kj)   ⊙ Fat – 10 g, of which less than 1 g saturated   ⊙ Sodium – 110 mg

NUTRITIONAL TIPS

Smoothies are a great way to increase your intake of soya protein. Use the recipe above with soya milk and a soya yogurt to give you 10 g of soya protein. There is 5 g in each 150 ml (¼ pint) soya milk and each 150 g (5 oz) soya yogurt.

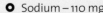

light 'n' low pancakes

1 Sift the flour into a bowl. If using wholemeal flour, also add the bran in the sieve to the flour in the bowl.

2 Beat the egg, milk and oil together, then slowly add to the flour. Stir the mixture until a smooth batter forms.

3 Leave to stand for about 20 minutes, then stir again.

4 Heat a little oil in a nonstick frying pan, or spray with an oil-water spray. When the oil is hot, add 2 tablespoons of the pancake mixture and shake the pan so that it spreads.

5 Cook the pancake for 2 minutes until the underside is lightly browned, then flip or turn over and cook the other side for a minute or so.

6 Keep the pancake warm in the oven while you cook the rest – you can stack one on top of the other as they are cooked. The mixture should make 8 pancakes in all. Serve with your chosen topping.

125 g (4 oz) brown or wholemeal plain flour

1 egg

300 ml (½ pint) skimmed milk (if using wholemeal flour you will need a little more)

1 teaspoon vegetable oil, plus a little extra for cooking, or use an oil-water spray (see page 23)

TOPPING IDEAS
chopped fresh fruit
chopped apple, raisins and ground cinnamon
cottage cheese
low-fat cream cheese
fruit spread or preserve

NUTRITIONAL FACTS* ● Kcals – 150 (630 Kj) ● Fat – 3 g, of which less than 1 g saturated ● Sodium – 60 mg

NUTRITIONAL TIPS
Pancakes offer another way in which you can base meals and snacks around starchy carbohydrates. They provide a good balance of many essential nutrients and can be low in fat if cooked with care.

* figures per serving – 2 pancakes, without topping

yogurt pots

1 Add one or more of the flavourings to the yogurt and stir to mix.

OR YOU COULD TRY...

Having fruit with your breakfast starts the day well. A one-portion 'fistful' of fruit will contain less than 1 g of fat and no more than 100 calories. So choose from these two tropical fruit combinations (2 servings), preparing the fruit as necessary and mixing with the fresh fruit juice:

1 mango, 2 pineapple slices, 1 kiwi fruit, 250 ml (8 fl oz) pineapple juice; or 4 passion fruit, 2 slices of melon, 1 nectarine, 250 ml (8 fl oz) passion fruit juice or tropical fruit juice

150 g (5 oz) natural yogurt or
    soya yogurt

FLAVOURING IDEAS

50 g (2 oz) rolled oats

3 tablespoons unsweetened
    breakfast cereal

1 tablespoon pine kernels, sunflower
    seeds or pumpkin seeds

1 tablespoon flaked almonds

1 tablespoon sultanas or raisins

1 piece fresh fruit, such as a chopped
    apple or sliced banana

50 g (2 oz) chopped fresh apricots
    or figs

1 small can peaches, pears or
    pineapple (in natural juice with no
    added sugar), drained and chopped

1 stewed or puréed apple with a
    sprinkling of ground cinnamon

50 g (2 oz) chopped dried fruit

NUTRITIONAL FACTS*    Kcals – 84 (353 Kj)   ● Fat – 2 g, of which less than 1 g saturated   ● Sodium – 125 mg

NUTRITIONAL TIPS
Yogurt is a superb skimmed-milk dairy product, providing rich creaminess without the fat of full-fat products. It is ideal for those still not quite awake at breakfast time, since it's easily digestible.

By adding any of the above flavourings to natural yogurt, you can avoid the extra fat and sugar that are added to some commercially prepared flavoured yogurts. Always remember to check the label (see page 30).

* figures per 150 g (5 oz) carton of natural yogurt

creamy porridge with summer berries

Preparation time: 5 minutes		Serves 2
Cooking time: 10–20 minutes		

1 Place the water and oats in a saucepan and bring to the boil. Simmer for 10–20 minutes, stirring occasionally.

2 Add the skimmed milk, stir and simmer for a few more minutes.

3 Serve with your chosen berries.

OR YOU COULD TRY...

Try sweetening your porridge with these other fruity combinations:

- blueberries, loganberries, blackcurrants or redcurrants
- raisins and sultanas
- apricots and figs
- bananas and walnuts
- prunes and a little honey

600 ml (1 pint) water

125 g (4 oz) porridge oats

150 ml (¼ pint) skimmed milk

1 handful fresh, frozen and thawed, canned or cooked berries, such as raspberries, strawberries, blackberries or cranberries

NUTRITIONAL FACTS 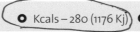 Kcals – 280 (1176 Kj), Fat – 6 g of fat, of which less than 1 g saturated Sodium – 60 mg

NUTRITIONAL TIPS
Oats provide one of the richest sources of the dietary soluble fibre beta-glucan. The recommended intake for a cholesterol-lowering effect is 3 g of beta-glucan per day, which will reduce your total cholesterol by 0.2 mmols/l (6 mg/dl). This bowl of porridge would reduce your cholesterol by 0.1 mmols/l (4 mg/dl) – modest I know, but it helps. Oats also have a low glycaemic index factor and therefore are useful for lowering the glycaemic index of the entire diet, to aid weight, glucose and cholesterol control.

pumpkin seed & apricot muesli

Preparation time: 10 minutes **Serves 2**

1 Place the oats, sultanas or raisins, seeds, almonds and apricots in a bowl with the fruit juice or water.

2 Add the grated apple and stir to mix.

3 Top with skimmed milk, soya milk, natural yogurt or soya yogurt.

OR YOU COULD TRY...
For a softer texture, soak the oats, sultanas and raisins with the fruit juice or water overnight.

50 g (2 oz) rolled jumbo oats

1 tablespoon sultanas or raisins

1 tablespoon pumpkin or sunflower seeds

1 tablespoon chopped almonds

25 g (1 oz) ready-to-eat dried apricots, chopped

2 tablespoons fruit juice, such as apple or orange juice, or water

2 small eating apples, peeled and grated

3 tablespoons skimmed milk, soya milk, natural yogurt or soya yogurt

NUTRITIONAL FACTS    ○ Kcals – 340 (1428 Kj)   ○ Fat – 12 g, of which 1 g saturated fat   ○ Sodium – 65 mg

NUTRITIONAL TIPS
Almonds and other nuts may help to lower your risk of heart disease. They are high in cardio-protective nutrients such as vitamin E, folate, magnesium, copper and arginine. Almonds are the richest nut source of vitamin E, one of the antioxidants which are believed to play a role in reducing the risk of heart disease by preventing the oxidation of LDL cholesterol. They also, like all nuts, have a high fat content but most of it is monounsaturated fat, so go easy if you are watching your waist measurement.

smoked mackerel and chive pâté

Preparation time: 10 minutes

Serves 8

1 Place the mackerel and cheese in a bowl and mash together well.

2 Add the remaining ingredients and mix well. Alternatively, mix all the ingredients together in a food processor or blender.

3 Spoon the mixture into 8 small individual serving dishes or 1 large serving dish or mould. Cover and refrigerate for at least 2 hours, or up to 4 hours. Serve the pâté chilled with vegetable batons (see page 46) and wholemeal toast, if liked.

200 g (7 oz) smoked mackerel, skinned, boned and flaked

125 g (4 oz) low-fat soft cheese

1 bunch of chives, chopped

1 tablespoon fat-free vinaigrette

1 tablespoon lemon juice

OR YOU COULD TRY...

Use other omega-3-rich fish instead of mackerel in this recipe, such as canned (in water or brine), drained pilchards, salmon or tuna.

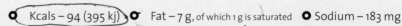

NUTRITIONAL FACTS · Kcals – 94 (395 kj) · Fat – 7 g, of which 1 g is saturated · Sodium – 183 mg

NUTRITIONAL TIPS SERVE 8

Of all the oily fish which are readily available, mackerel is the richest source of omega-3 fatty acids, so enjoy it in all its many forms – fresh, canned or smoked. It is also one of the least expensive oily fish.

tahini hummus

1 Place the chickpeas, tahini, garlic, lemon juice and cumin in a food processor or blender. Process until well blended, adding a little water or vegetable stock if you prefer a thinner consistency. Taste and add more garlic, lemon juice or cumin to your liking.

2 Transfer the hummus to a serving bowl. Sprinkle with paprika or chopped parsley. Serve with vegetable batons (see page 46) and Pitta Bread Crisps (see below) or Turkish bread. Or use as an alternative to spread on bread.

SERVE WITH...

Pitta bread crisps: cut a pitta bread, either wholemeal or white, into quarters or eighths. Split and separate each piece into two. Spread the pieces in a single layer on a nonstick baking sheet. Bake in a preheated oven, 150°C (300°F), Gas Mark 2, for 10–15 minutes, until the pieces of bread are dried out and crisp.

250 g (8 oz) canned chickpeas, rinsed and drained

2 tablespoons tahini (sesame seed paste)

3 garlic cloves, chopped

125 ml (4 fl oz) lemon juice

pinch of ground cumin

Vegetable Stock (see page 138) or water (optional)

paprika or chopped parsley, to garnish

NUTRITIONAL FACTS   ○ Kcals – 88 (370 kj) ○ Fat – 5 g, of which 0.6 g saturates ○ Sodium – 93 mg

NUTRITIONAL TIPS  SERVE 6 –

This hummus recipe is low in fat because it is oil free. Tahini is used instead of the customary olive oil and the final product is smooth, lemony and light. Accompany the hummus with the suggested pitta bread crisps instead of normal crisps and see what a saving you can make: Pitta Bread Crisps (per serving) contain: 50 Kcals, less than 1 g of fat, of which negligible is saturated fat, 100 mg sodium. Potato crisps (per individual packet) contain: 159 Kcals 10 g of fat, of which 4 g is saturated and 252 mg sodium.

red pepper & spring onion dip with vegetable batons

Preparation time: 10 minutes

Cooking time: 30–40 minutes

 (V)

Serves 4

1 Slightly flatten the pepper quarters and place on a baking sheet. Wrap the garlic in foil and place on the sheet. Roast in a preheated oven, 220°C (425°F), Gas Mark 7, for 30–40 minutes until the pepper is slightly charred and the garlic is soft.

2 When cool enough to handle, remove the skin from the pepper and discard. Transfer the flesh to a bowl.

3 Squeeze the roasted garlic flesh from the cloves into the bowl.

4 Using a fork, roughly mash the pepper and garlic together. Stir in the soya yogurt and spring onions. Season to taste with pepper. Serve with the vegetable batons.

1 large red pepper, cut into quarters, cored and deseeded

2 garlic cloves, unpeeled

250 g (8 oz) soya yogurt

2 spring onions, finely chopped

freshly ground black pepper

selection of raw vegetables, such as carrots, cucumber, peppers, fennel, tomatoes, baby corn, mangetout, celery and courgettes, cut into batons, to serve

NUTRITIONAL FACTS* (Kcals – 60 (252 Kj)) ● Fat – 1 g of fat, of which less than 0.5 g saturated ● Sodium – 2 mg

NUTRITIONAL TIPS

This soya dip will provide you with 2 g soya protein. Research has shown that a daily intake of 25 g soya protein per day can significantly reduce total as well as LDL cholesterol (the 'bad guy') as part of a healthy diet.

* figures for the dip only

spicy lentil & tomato soup

Preparation time: 20 minutes
Cooking time: 40–50 minutes

 V

Serves 4

1 Heat the oil in a large saucepan, add the onion, garlic and chilli (if using) and fry gently for 4–5 minutes until soft.

2 Add the lentils, bay leaf, celery, carrots, leek and stock. Cover and bring to the boil, then reduce the heat and simmer for 30–40 minutes until the lentils are soft. Remove the bay leaf.

3 Stir in the tomatoes, tomato purée, turmeric, ginger, coriander and pepper to taste. Allow to cool a little, then transfer to a food processor or blender. Process until smooth, adding more stock or water if necessary.

4 Reheat gently, before serving with a swirl of yogurt. Serve with crusty wholemeal bread, if liked.

1 tablespoon vegetable oil

1 large onion, finely chopped

2 garlic cloves, finely chopped

1 small green chilli, deseeded and finely chopped (optional)

250 g (8 oz) red lentils, washed and drained

1 bay leaf

3 celery sticks, thinly sliced

3 carrots, thinly sliced

1 leek, thinly sliced

1.5 litres (2½ pints) Vegetable Stock (see page 138)

400 g (13 oz) can chopped tomatoes

2 tablespoons tomato purée

½ teaspoon ground turmeric

½ teaspoon ground ginger

1 tablespoon chopped fresh coriander

freshly ground black pepper

natural yogurt, to garnish

NUTRITIONAL FACTS   ● Kcals – 288 (1210 Kj) ● Fat – 2 g, of which less than 1 g saturated ● Sodium – 117 mg

NUTRITIONAL TIPS   SERVE 4
All pulses – beans, peas and lentils – are high in soluble fibre, which is good for cholesterol reduction. They also add satisfying power to a soup, and this lentil soup is particularly filling!

sweet potato & butternut squash soup

1 Heat the oil in a large saucepan and add the onion and garlic. Cover and cook very gently for 10 minutes, without colouring.

2 Add the spices, ginger, chilli, lime rind and honey and stir for 30 seconds, then add the sweet potato, squash, half the lime juice and the stock.

3 Cover and bring to the boil. Reduce the heat and simmer for about 10 minutes until the vegetables are almost tender. Stir in the chickpeas. Check the seasoning and add pepper to taste. Simmer for a further 10 minutes, then add the remaining lime juice to taste.

4 Allow to cool slightly, then process in a food processor or blender until very smooth, adding more stock if necessary to achieve the desired consistency. Reheat gently and stir in the fresh coriander just before serving.

1 tablespoon vegetable oil

1 onion, finely chopped

2 garlic cloves, finely chopped

1 teaspoon cumin seeds

1 teaspoon ground coriander

1 cm (½ inch) piece of fresh root ginger, peeled and finely grated

1 green chilli, deseeded and finely chopped

finely grated rind and juice of 1 lime

1 teaspoon honey

375 g (12 oz) sweet potatoes, peeled and cut into small chunks

375 g (12 oz) butternut squash, peeled and cut into small chunks

1.2 litres (2 pints) Vegetable Stock (see page 138)

250 g (8 oz) canned chickpeas, rinsed and drained

handful of fresh coriander leaves, chopped

NUTRITIONAL FACTS   ● Kcals – 260 (1092 Kj) ● Fat – 6 g, of which less than 1 g saturated   ● Sodium – 206 mg

NUTRITIONAL TIPS SERVE 4
Butternut squash is a large, pear-shaped squash with a hard, inedible rind, orange flesh and a slightly sweet, buttery and nutty flavour – hence the name! It is high in antioxidant vitamins, especially beta-carotene, which gives it its lovely colour. Squash is a versatile vegetable and can be roasted with olive oil and thyme or added to casseroles, soups and stews. It is also good for desserts, since it has a sweet flavour, and is great baked with apple, cinnamon, brown sugar and ground ginger.

fennel & white bean soup

1 Place 300 ml (½ pint) of the stock in a large saucepan. Add the fennel, onion, courgette, carrot and garlic. Cover and bring to the boil. Continue boiling for 5 minutes, then remove the lid, reduce the heat and simmer gently for about 20 minutes until the vegetables are tender.

2 Stir in the tomatoes, beans and sage. Season to taste with pepper and pour in the remaining stock. Simmer for five minutes, then allow the soup to cool slightly.

3 Transfer 300 ml (½ pint) of the soup to a food processor or blender and process until smooth. Stir back into the pan and heat through gently.

900 ml (1½ pints) Vegetable Stock
   (see page 138)
2 fennel bulbs, trimmed and
   chopped
1 onion, chopped
1 courgette, chopped
1 carrot, chopped
2 garlic cloves, finely sliced
6 tomatoes, finely chopped, or
   400 g (13 oz) can tomatoes
2 x 400 g (13 oz) cans butter beans,
   rinsed and drained
2 tablespoons chopped sage
freshly ground black pepper

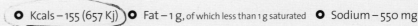

NUTRITIONAL FACTS   ● Kcals – 155 (657 Kj) ● Fat – 1 g, of which less than 1 g saturated   ● Sodium – 550 mg

NUTRITIONAL TIPS   SERVE 4
When choosing canned vegetables, go for the 'no added salt' varieties. If these aren't available, rinse and drain vegetables such as beans and sweetcorn. This removes some but not all of the salt.

crispy potato skins

1 Scrub the potatoes and place in a preheated oven, 220°C (425°F), Gas Mark 7, for 1¼ hours until tender. Alternatively prick the potatoes and place on kitchen paper in the microwave and cook on maximum (100%) for 6 minutes, turn and cook for a further 7 minutes, or follow the instructions in your handbook.

2 Halve the potatoes, scoop out the insides, leaving a shell about 6 mm (¼ inch) thick. (Save the scooped-out potato for another use, such as for a root mash or in a soup.) Cut each of the shells in half lengthways.

3 Spray a nonstick baking sheet with oil-water spray. Place the potato quarters, skin side down, on the sheet and spray lightly with oil-water spray. Bake in a preheated oven, 200°C (400°F), Gas Mark 6, for 25–35 minutes until golden brown and very crisp. Serve immediately.

OR YOU COULD TRY...

They are great on their own with just a shower of black pepper and a squeeze of fresh lemon juice, with dips such as Tahini Hummus (see page 45), or Red Pepper and Spring Onion Dip (see page 46). Alternatively, they can also be served as a vegetable accompaniment to meat, poultry or fish dishes when you want a potato dish with a crisp texture.

2 large baking potatoes
oil-water spray (see page 23)

NUTRITIONAL FACTS   ○ Kcals – 115 (483 kj) ○ Fat – less than 1 g, of which negligible saturated ○ Sodium – 10 mg

NUTRITIONAL TIPS   SERVE 2.
By using the oil-water spray, these potato skins become a really low-fat snack compared to the conventional version which is usually topped with crispy bacon and cheese and smothered in sour cream.

garlic, pea & parmesan crostini

Preparation time: 25 minutes
Cooking time: 55 minutes

Serves 8

1 Roast the garlic following the method for Garlic Mash (see page 88).

2 Meanwhile, to make the crostini, cut the loaf into 40 slices about ½–1 cm (¼–½ inch) thick. Using an oil-water spray or pastry brush, lightly coat each side of the bread slices with oil.

3 Place the bread slices on a rack and bake in a preheated oven, 200°C (400°F), Gas Mark 6, for about 5–10 minutes, turning the bread over as it turns pale gold. Remove and allow to cool.

4 Cook the peas in boiling water until tender. Drain and transfer to a food processor or blender or mash in a bowl with a fork. Separate the garlic cloves, squeeze out the roasted garlic flesh and add to the peas with the spread and Parmesan. Process or mash to a creamy purée. Allow to cool before spreading on to the crostini. Garnish with parsley or mint, if liked.

1 head of garlic

1 French baguette

olive oil-water spray (see page 23) or a little olive oil

200 g (7 oz) frozen peas

1 tablespoon unsaturated spread

2 tablespoons freshly grated Parmesan cheese

1 tablespoon chopped mint

parsley to garnish

OTHER CROSTINI TOPPINGS

Reduced-fat soft cheese and prawns

Red or green pesto sauce

Green olive paste

Smoked Mackerel and Chive Pâté (see page 44)

Goats' cheese

Tahini Hummus (see page 45)

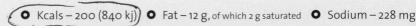

NUTRITIONAL FACTS ● Kcals – 200 (840 kj) ● Fat – 12 g, of which 2 g saturated ● Sodium – 228 mg

NUTRITIONAL TIPS   SERVE 4
Crostini, made with olive oil, follow the beneficial Mediterranean diet rule for a starter or snack. Olive oil is a rich source of monounsaturates and vitamin E. Add lots of vegetables to the toppings for extra antioxidant nutrients.

mediterranean vegetable & walnut salad

Preparation time: 30 minutes   v   **Serves 6**

1 Heat the walnuts in a dry pan over a medium heat for 1–2 minutes until slightly toasted.

2 Whisk together the olive vinaigrette and olives in a small bowl .

3 Mix together the chickpeas, pepper, carrot and onion in a medium bowl. Toss with 3 tablespoons of the vinaigrette.

4 Toss the spinach and other salad leaves with the remaining vinaigrette. Transfer to a large serving bowl, top with the vegetable mixture and sprinkle with walnuts.

75 g (3 oz) walnuts, chopped

75 ml (3 fl oz) Olive Vinaigrette
  (see page 139)

1 tablespoon pitted olives

400 g (13 oz) can chickpeas

1 red pepper, cored, deseeded and
  thinly sliced

1 large carrot, cut into matchsticks

1 small red onion, thinly sliced

4 handfuls of baby spinach

4 handfuls of green salad leaves

NUTRITIONAL FACTS    Kcals – 300 (1260 Kj)   ○ Fat – 13 g, of which 1 g saturated   ○ Sodium – 550 mg

NUTRITIONAL TIPS SERVE 6
Walnuts are one of the richest plant sources of omega-3 fatty acids available. A handful of walnuts provides as much omega-3 as a 75 g (3 oz) portion of salmon. Walnut oil is also rich in omega-3.

oriental-style coleslaw

Preparation time: 20 minutes   V   **Serves 6**

1 Place all the salad ingredients in a large serving bowl and toss them well to combine.

2 For the dressing, heat the sesame seeds in a small, dry saucepan over a medium heat, shaking the pan frequently for 2–3 minutes until toasted.

3 Stir in the remaining dressing ingredients. Remove the pan from heat, immediately pour the dressing over the salad. Toss to combine.

OR YOU COULD TRY...

Vary the coleslaw recipe above by substituting or adding one or more of the following ingredients: white cabbage, fennel, celery, onions, apples, oranges, sunflower seeds, pumpkin seeds, dried fruit, such as sultanas, raisins and ready-to-eat apricots, walnuts, pine nuts, garlic, fresh herbs.

1 white radish, cut into long, thin strips

1 large carrot, cut into long, thin strips

½ Chinese cabbage, shredded

¼ red cabbage, shredded

2 spring onions, cut into long, thin strips

18 mangetout, cut lengthways into thin, strips

50 g (2 oz) spinach, shredded

50 g (2 oz) fresh or dried figs, cut lengthways into quarters

75 g (3 oz) flaked almonds

DRESSING

2 tablespoons sesame seeds

3 teaspoons grated fresh root ginger

1 teaspoon sugar

3 tablespoons sherry or rice wine vinegar

2 teaspoons peanut oil

2 teaspoons reduced-salt soy sauce

a few drops of sesame oil (optional)

NUTRITIONAL FACTS   Kcals – 160 (672 Kj)   Fat – 10 g, of which 1 g saturated   Sodium – 35 mg

NUTRITIONAL TIPS   Serve 6.

Standard ready-prepared coleslaw contains mayonnaise and is therefore high in fat, but reduced-fat varieties are available, so check the label. There is also a range of perfectly acceptable fat-free dressings now available .

baked beetroot, spinach & orange salad

Preparation time: 20 minutes
Cooking time: 1–2 hours

V   **Serves 4**

1 To bake the beetroot, place the whole beetroots on a piece of foil large enough to enclose loosely with the garlic and oregano. Season to taste with pepper and drizzle over the oil and vinegar.

2 Gather up the foil loosely and fold over at the top to seal. Place on a baking sheet and bake in a preheated oven, 200°C (400°F), Gas Mark 6, for 1–2 hours, depending on size of the beetroot, until tender.

3 Remove from the oven and allow them to cool before peeling and slicing the beetroot. Discard the garlic.

4 Place the spinach in a layer in the bottom of a large salad bowl followed by alternate layers of beetroot and orange.

5 Drizzle over the dressing and season with pepper to taste. Garnish with oregano.

500 g (1 lb) raw whole beetroots,
    preferably of even size
2 garlic cloves
handful of oregano leaves
1 teaspoon olive oil
1 tablespoon balsamic vinegar
200 g (7 oz) baby spinach
2 oranges, segmented
5 tablespoons Olive Vinaigrette
    (see page 139)
freshly ground black pepper
chopped oregano, to garnish

OR YOU COULD TRY...

The baked beetroot is also delicious served hot as a vegetable accompaniment to meat and fish, or roughly mashed to a purée, in which case the garlic it is baked with can be added to the mash.

NUTRITIONAL FACTS   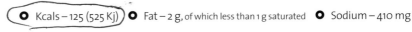 ● Kcals – 125 (525 Kj) ● Fat – 2 g, of which less than 1 g saturated ● Sodium – 410 mg

NUTRITIONAL TIPS *SERVE 4*
Beetroot is important for heart health as it contains a high amount of antioxidants, as indicated by its vibrant colour. It also contains other beneficial vitamins and minerals including beta-carotene, vitamins B6 and C, folic acid, manganese, calcium, magnesium, iron, potassium and phosphorous – all important for heart health. Beetroot has a sweet taste and yet is surprisingly low in calories – weight for weight, it contains fewer than an apple.

tabbouleh

Preparation time: 15 minutes, plus standing   v   **Serves 6**

1 Place the bulgar wheat in a bowl. Pour over boiling water to cover and leave to stand for 45–60 minutes until the grains swell and soften.

2 Drain and press to remove excess moisture. Place in a salad bowl. Add the onion, tomatoes, cucumber, parsley and mint. Toss to combine.

3 For the dressing, place the ingredients in a screw-top jar, replace the lid and shake well to combine. Pour over the salad and toss to coat. Cover and refrigerate until ready to use – within 2–3 days.

OR YOU COULD TRY...
Tabbouleh is highly versatile and makes an ideal accompaniment for fish and meat dishes, such as Orange and Cider Poached Mackerel (see page 81), or Turkish Lamb and Potato Stew (see page 121). It is also tasty as a baked potato topping or as a filling for pitta bread.

175 g (6 oz) bulgar wheat

300 ml (½ pint) boiling water

1 red onion, finely chopped

3 tomatoes, diced

¼ cucumber, chopped

10 tablespoons chopped parsley

5 tablespoons chopped mint

DRESSING
100 ml (3½ fl oz) lemon juice

2 teaspoons olive oil

freshly ground black pepper

NUTRITIONAL FACTS   **⊙ Kcals – 134 (563 Kj)**   ⊙ Fat – 22 g, of which a less than 1 g saturated   ⊙ Sodium – 8 mg

NUTRITIONAL TIPS *SERVE 6*
Tabbouleh is a Middle Eastern dish that has become a popular salad choice worldwide, and there are many delicious varieties. The reduced-fat dressing in this version makes a healthy dish even healthier. During milling, bulgar wheat is cracked rather than ground and therefore the grain remains as a whole grain, retaining the valuable nutrients in the germ and bran. The glycaemic index (GI) of bulgar wheat is low, which helps to reduce the GI of the whole diet.

three bean & tuna salad

Preparation time: 15 minutes
Cooking time: 5 minutes

Serves 6

1 If using fresh or frozen French beans, lightly cook for 4–5 minutes in boiling water, or steam or microwave. Refresh under cold running water, then drain well.

2 Flake the tuna and place in a bowl with all the beans and the onion.

3 Mix together the dressing ingredients and pour over the bean and tuna mixture.

4 Toss lightly and garnish with olives. Serve on a bed of salad leaves.

175 g (6 oz) French beans, canned, fresh or frozen
200 g (7 oz) can tuna, rinsed and drained
175 g (6 oz) canned butter beans, rinsed and drained
175 g (6 oz) canned red kidney beans, rinsed and drained
1 onion, finely sliced
12 olives, to garnish
salad leaves, to serve

DRESSING
1 teaspoon Dijon mustard
2 tablespoons balsamic vinegar
1 tablespoon olive oil
1 tablespoon tomato purée
1 small garlic clove, crushed
2 tablespoons chopped parsley
pinch of dried basil or oregano
freshly ground black pepper

NUTRITIONAL FACTS    Kcals – 130 (546 Kj) ❍ Fat – 3 g, of which less than 1 g saturated ❍ Sodium – 560 mg

NUTRITIONAL TIPS    SERVE 6

This dish is full of beans, which are abundant in cardio-protective nutrients. They are deliciously combined with low-fat canned tuna. Served with a Mediterranean-style dressing, this salad is a healthy complement to any meal.

orange & almond couscous salad

Preparation time: 15 minutes, plus standing
Cooking time: 5 minutes

v   **Serves 6**

1 Place the apple juice in a saucepan and bring to the boil. Slowly stir in the couscous. Remove the pan from heat. Cover and leave to stand for 10 minutes. Fluff up with a fork.

2 Add the pepper, herbs and currants to the couscous. Toss to combine. Transfer to a serving bowl. Scatter with the orange segments and onion.

3 For the dressing, place the ingredients in a small saucepan and heat gently to dissolve the honey – do not allow to boil. Drizzle over the salad. Scatter with the almonds.

250 ml (8 fl oz) apple juice

175 g (6 oz) couscous

½ red pepper, cored, deseeded and diced

4 tablespoons chopped parsley

3 tablespoons chopped mint

25 g (1 oz) currants

2 oranges, segmented

1 red onion, sliced

25 g (1 oz) flaked almonds

DRESSING

juice of 1 orange

juice of 1 lemon or lime

2 teaspoons olive or hazelnut oil

1 teaspoon honey

NUTRITIONAL FACTS    **O** Kcals – 160 (672 Kj) **O** Fat – 4 g, of which 0.3 g saturated **O** Sodium – 6 mg

NUTRITIONAL TIPS   SERVE
Almonds (see also the Nutritional Tip on page 42) contain the amino acid arginine (amongst other vital nutrients), thought to improve the health of artery linings and reduce the risk of heart disease.

caponata ratatouille

Preparation time: 20 minutes

Cooking time: 40 minutes

v

Serves 6

1 Cut the aubergines and onions into 1 cm (½ inch) chunks.

2 Heat the oil in a nonstick frying pan until very hot, add the aubergine and fry for about 15 minutes until very soft. Add a little boiling water to prevent sticking if necessary.

3 Meanwhile, place the onion and celery in a saucepan with a little water or wine. Cook for 5 minutes until tender but still firm.

4 Add the tomatoes, thyme, cayenne pepper and aubergine and onions. Cook for 15 minutes, stirring occasionally.

5 Add the capers, olives, wine vinegar, sugar and cocoa powder (if using) and cook for 2–3 minutes. Season with pepper and serve garnished with almonds and parsley. Serve hot or cold as a side dish, starter or a main dish. Serve with polenta and hot crusty bread, if liked.

750 g (1½ lb) aubergines

1 large Spanish onion

1 tablespoon olive oil

3 celery sticks, coarsely chopped

a little wine (optional)

2 large beef tomatoes, skinned and
  deseeded

1 teaspoon chopped thyme

¼–½ teaspoon cayenne pepper

2 tablespoons capers

handful of pitted green olives

4 tablespoons wine vinegar

1 tablespoon sugar

1–2 tablespoons cocoa powder
  (optional)

freshly ground black pepper

TO GARNISH

toasted, chopped almonds

chopped parsley

NUTRITIONAL FACTS   ● Kcals – 90 (378 Kj)   ● Fat – 4 g, of which 1 g saturated   ● Sodium – 155 mg

NUTRITIONAL TIPS   SERVE 6

Aubergines can absorb a lot of fat when fried and therefore it is important to measure the amount of olive oil and not be tempted to add any more. Instead of using oil, you can sauté vegetables in wine, water or stock with tasty results.

spiced roast roots

Preparation time: 20 minutes
Cooking time: 40 minutes

V   **Serves 6**

1 Place all the vegetables and garlic in a large roasting tin. Sprinkle over the crushed seeds and squeeze over the ginger pulp to extract the juice. Season to taste with pepper and drizzle over the oil.

2 Roast in a preheated oven, 200°C (400°F), Gas Mark 6, for 30 minutes, stirring occasionally.

3 Pour over the wine and return to the oven for a further 10 minutes. Garnish with parsley. Serve as a side dish or as a main meal, with fresh baked bread toasted with a topping of reduced-fat cheese.

4 carrots, thickly sliced diagonally

250 g (8 oz) swede, cubed

250 g (8 oz) sweet potato, cubed

1 onion, cut into 8 wedges

2 leeks, thickly sliced diagonally

6 garlic cloves

½ teaspoon mustard or cumin
   seeds, lightly crushed

½ teaspoon coriander seeds,
   lightly crushed

2 cm (1 inch) piece fresh root ginger,
   peeled and finely grated

1 tablespoon olive oil

100 ml (3½ fl oz) dry white wine

freshly ground black pepper

1 tablespoon flat leaf parsley,
   to garnish

NUTRITIONAL FACTS   Kcals – 100 (420 Kj)   Fat – 3 g, of which less than 1 g saturated   Sodium – 30 mg

NUTRITIONAL TIPS   SERVE 6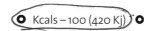
Garlic is thought to be good for your heart but not enough scientific trials have yet been carried out to confirm the benefits. It certainly contains a substance called allicin, which dilates the blood vessels and reduces blood clotting.

NUTRITIONAL FACTS ○ Kcals – 192 (806 Kj) ○ Fat – 5 g, of which less than 1 g saturated ○ Sodium – 34 mg

NUTRITIONAL TIPS SERVE 4

Fish is a good low-fat option: monkfish, sole, cod, halibut, haddock, hake, red snapper, mullet, plaice, pollock, trout, turbot and whiting all have fewer than 5 g of fat per 100 g. When you eat out, try and choose fish from the menu.

crab & coriander cakes

Preparation time: 25–30 minutes
Cooking time: 10 minutes

Serves 6

1 In a large bowl, mix together the crab meat, mashed potatoes, coriander, spring onions, lemon rind and juice and half the beaten egg to bind.

2 Form the mixture into 12 cakes about 1 cm (½ inch) thick. Coat the cakes with flour, then dip into the remaining egg and then the breadcrumbs.

3 Heat the oil in a nonstick frying pan and fry the cakes for about 10 minutes until golden, turning once or twice.

4 Drain on kitchen paper before serving. Serve with a sweet red chilli sauce, or Tomato Salsa (see page 141).

OR YOU COULD TRY...

You can make lots of variations on this recipe, for example using canned tuna or salmon, or fresh fish, or adding peas or sweetcorn. Try making a vegetable version using peas, broccoli and carrots instead of fish.

375 g (12 oz) canned crab meat, drained
250 g (8 oz) cold mashed potatoes
2 tablespoons chopped fresh coriander
1 bunch of spring onions, finely sliced
grated rind and juice of ½ lemon
2 eggs, beaten
flour, for coating
150 g (5 oz) fresh white breadcrumbs
1 tablespoon oil

NUTRITIONAL FACTS   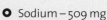 Kcals – 185 (777 Kj) ● Fat – 5 g, of which 1 g saturated ● Sodium – 509 mg

NUTRITIONAL TIPS   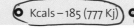 SERVE 6

Canned crab meat contains a moderate amount of omega-3 fatty acids (0.91 g omega-3 per 100 g). Canned fish is saltier than fresh fish (unless it is canned in water), so lower the salt content by putting the fish in a sieve or colander and rinsing it under cold running water. Drain thoroughly on kitchen paper. You can use this tip when you are preparing any canned fish or beans, whether they are canned in oil, brine, salt or sugar. Just put them under the tap and rinse away the unwanted extras.

parsley & garlic marinated sardines

Preparation time: 10 minutes
Cooking time: 5 minutes

Serves 6

1 Place all the ingredients for the marinade in a small saucepan. Bring to the boil, then remove from the heat.

2 Place the sardines on a prepared barbecue or on a preheated hot griddle or under a hot grill. Cook for 1–2 minutes on each side until crisp and golden.

3 Place the sardines in a single layer in a shallow dish. Pour the dressing over the sardines and serve hot. Alternatively, cover and refrigerate for at least 1 hour before serving cold. Serve with Tabbouleh (see page 60) and a mixed green leaf salad, if liked.

OR YOU COULD TRY...

Drain a can of sardines and place in a food processor with 1 crushed garlic clove, 1 tablespoon drained capers, 6 pitted olives, some chopped parsley and 1 tablespoon of wine or balsamic vinegar. Process until blended. Spread on piping hot toast for a delicious snack or starter.

12 fresh sardines, cleaned, or use
   fillets if preferred

MARINADE

50 g (2 oz) chopped parsley
**1 teaspoon freshly ground
   black pepper**
1 garlic clove, crushed
**finely grated rind and juice of
   1 lemon**
2 tablespoons white wine
1 tablespoon olive oil

NUTRITIONAL FACTS   ◉ Kcals – 180 (756 Kj) ◉ Fat – 10 g, of which 2.5g saturated ◉ Sodium – 112 mg

NUTRITIONAL TIPS SERVE 6
A 100 g (3½ oz) portion of fresh sardines contains 2.7 g of omega-3 fatty acids. This Mediterranean recipe is equally suitable for other types of fish that are high in omega-3 fatty acids (see page 22), such as mackerel and salmon.

Make eating fish two or three times a week a delicious and easy choice by eating simple snacks such as sardines on toast as well as choosing a variety of different types of fish for your main meals.

puy lentils with flaked salmon & dill

Preparation time: 30 minutes

Cooking time: 45 minutes

Serves 4

1 Place the salmon on a sheet of foil and spoon over the wine. Gather up the foil and fold over at the top to seal. Place on a baking sheet and bake in a preheated oven, 200°C (400°F), Gas Mark 6, for 15–20 minutes until cooked. Allow to cool, then flake, cover and chill.

2 Flatten the pepper halves slightly. Grill skin side up under a preheated hot grill until charred. Enclose in a plastic bag for a few minutes. Remove from the bag, peel away the skin and cut the flesh into 2.5 cm (1 inch) cubes, reserving any juices.

3 Place all the dressing ingredients, except the oil, in a food processor or blender and process until smooth. Whilst processing, drizzle in the oil until the mixture is thick.

4 Place the lentils in a large saucepan with plenty of water, bring to the boil, then simmer gently for about 15–20 minutes until cooked but still firm to the bite. Drain and place in a bowl with the pepper, dill, most of the spring onions and pepper to taste.

5 Stir the dressing into the hot lentils and allow to infuse. To serve, top the lentils with the flaked salmon and gently mix through the lentils and dressing, squeeze over a little lemon juice and scatter with the remaining spring onions.

500 g (1 lb) salmon tail fillet

2 tablespoons dry white wine

4 red peppers, halved, cored and deseeded

175 g (6 oz) Puy lentils, well rinsed

large handful of dill, chopped

1 bunch of spring onions, finely sliced

lemon juice, for squeezing

freshly ground black pepper

DRESSING

2 garlic cloves

large handful of flat leaf parsley, chopped

large handful of dill, chopped

1 teaspoon Dijon mustard

2 green chillies, deseeded and chopped

juice of 2 large lemons

1 tablespoon extra virgin olive oil

NUTRITIONAL TIPS   SERVE 4

As well as making a delicious and unusual flavour combination, lentils and salmon make an excellent cardio-protective duo. Lentils are high in protein, low in fat and high in soluble fibre, which will help reduce cholesterol levels. Salmon is an oily fish, providing a rich source of omega-3 fatty acids, which will have a beneficial effect on reducing blood clotting and an irregular heartbeat. Canned salmon is also a good source of omega-3 fatty acids but has a higher salt content than fresh salmon.

chilli & coriander fish parcels

Preparation time: 15 minutes, plus marinating
Cooking time: 15 minutes

Serves 1

1 Place the fish in a non-metallic dish and sprinkle with lemon juice. Cover and leave in the refrigerator to marinate for 15–20 minutes.

2 Place the coriander, garlic and chilli in a food processor or blender and process until the mixture forms a paste. Add the sugar and yogurt and briefly process to blend.

3 Place the fish on a sheet of foil. Coat the fish on both sides with the paste. Gather up the foil loosely and turn over at the top to seal. Return to the refrigerator for at least 1 hour.

4 Place the parcel on a baking tray and bake in a preheated oven, 200°C (400°F), Gas Mark 6, for about 15 minutes until the fish is just cooked.

OR YOU COULD TRY...
Simply combine, for example, chicken, steak or salmon with your favourite vegetables and herbs and bake in foil to provide a flavourful dish complete with its own homemade sauce.

125 g (4 oz) cod, coley or haddock
   fillet
2 teaspoons lemon juice
1 tablespoon fresh coriander leaves
1 garlic clove
1 green chilli, deseeded and
   chopped
¼ teaspoon sugar
2 teaspoons natural yogurt

NUTRITIONAL FACTS   Kcals – 127 (533 Kj)   Fat – 1 g, of which 0.2g saturated   Sodium – 90 mg

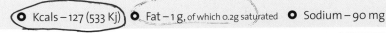

NUTRITIONAL TIPS   SERVE 1
Cod is a low-fat white fish, a good source of protein and a useful source of iron. It has only 0.3 g omega-3 fatty acids per 125 g (4 oz) portion, but nevertheless will still make a contribution to your omega-3 intake. People who eat fish regularly are less likely to die of heart disease than those who rarely or never eat it. There is an association between eating any type of fish 2–3 times per week (averaging out at 20–50 g/¾–2 oz per day) and a lowered risk of cardiovascular diseases.

tuna & mixed vegetable pasta bake

Preparation time: 10 minutes
Cooking time: 30 minutes

Serves 4

1 Heat the oil in a nonstick frying pan, add the onion and fry for about 5 minutes until soft.

2 Meanwhile, cook the macaroni according to the packet instructions, until just tender. Drain.

3 Mix the pasta with the onion, tuna, tomatoes, vegetables, cottage cheese and fromage frais or yogurt. Pour into a greased casserole or ovenproof dish. Top with the breadcrumbs.

4 Bake in a preheated oven, 180°C (350°F), Gas Mark 4, for about 30 minutes until golden on top. Serve with a mixed salad and Potato & Olive Bread (see page 86), if liked.

1 tablespoon vegetable oil

1 onion, chopped

250 g (8 oz) wholemeal macaroni

200 g (7 oz) can tuna, well drained and flaked

400 g (13 oz) can tomatoes

125 g (4 oz) cooked mixed frozen vegetables

125 g (4 oz) cottage cheese with chives

2 tablespoons natural fromage frais or yogurt

75 g (3 oz) wholemeal breadcrumbs

NUTRITIONAL FACTS ● Kcals – 400 (1680 Kj) ● Fat – 6 g, of which 1 g saturated ● Sodium – 425 mg

NUTRITIONAL TIPS *Serve 4*
Canned tuna contains fewer omega-3 fatty acids than fresh tuna and other canned forms of oily fish because much of the fat is lost when it is pre-cooked before canning. This does not happen to the more oil-rich salmon, mackerel, sardines or pilchards. Nevertheless, canned tuna is a very useful low-fat and low-calorie fish, so keep some in your storecupboard for pasta bakes, sandwiches, salads, baked potatoes and sauces. Tuna canned in spring water is the best variety to buy.

griddled honey-glazed tuna with parsnip purée

Preparation time: 15 minutes

Cooking time: 15 minutes

Serves 4

1 Place the ingredients for the glaze in a small saucepan. Bring to the boil, then reduce the heat and simmer until the mixture reduces and is of a glaze consistency. Keep hot.

2 For the parsnip purée, steam the parsnips and potatoes until tender. Drain if necessary and place in a food processor or blender with the yogurt, horseradish (if using) and pepper to taste. Process until blended. Keep warm or reheat prior to serving.

3 Brush the tuna with oil. Cook on a preheated, very hot griddle or barbecue, or in a frying pan or under a grill, for 1–2 minutes. Turn and spoon the glaze over the tuna. Cook for a further 1–2 minutes – it's best if moist and still slightly pink in the centre.

4 To serve, top a mound of the purée with a tuna steak and spoon over the remaining glaze. Accompany with steamed green vegetables, if liked.

4 tuna steaks, about 125 g (4 oz) each

2 teaspoons olive oil

GLAZE

1 tablespoon honey

2 tablespoons wholegrain mustard

1 teaspoon tomato purée

2 tablespoons orange juice

1 tablespoon red wine vinegar or balsamic vinegar

freshly ground black pepper

PARSNIP PURÉE

2 parsnips, cut into chunks

2 potatoes, cut into chunks

50 g (2 oz) natural yogurt

2 teaspoons horseradish relish (optional)

NUTRITIONAL FACTS Kcals – 310 (1302 Kj) Fat – 10 g, of which 2 g saturated Sodium – 300 mg

NUTRITIONAL TIPS ~~Serve 4~~
Griddling is a healthy way to cook, since it requires little or no added fat, and any fat from the food can drain away. Griddle pans can be heated to a very high heat, which gives food a delicious flavour and helps to seal in all the juices.

cod with chilli butter beans & tomatoes

Preparation time: 15 minutes

Cooking time: 20 minutes

Serves 4

1 Heat the oil in a nonstick saucepan and add the celery, onion and garlic. Cook for about 5 minutes until softened. Add the tomatoes, tomato purée, beans and chilli. Simmer, uncovered, for 10 minutes.

2 Meanwhile, heat the wine in a separate saucepan. Add the fish and poach gently for about 3–4 minutes until just cooked through.

3 Combine the undrained fish with the bean and tomato mixture and heat through. Add pepper to taste and garnish with parsley. Serve with new potatoes, basmati rice or pasta and dark green spinach or broccoli for a feast of colour.

2 teaspoons vegetable oil

1 celery stick, finely diced

1 onion, finely chopped

1 garlic clove, crushed, or 1 teaspoon minced garlic

400 g (13 oz) can tomatoes, undrained and mashed

2 tablespoons tomato purée

300 g (10 oz) can butter beans, well drained

1 green chilli, deseeded and finely chopped

125 ml (4 fl oz) dry white wine

500 g (1 lb) cod fillet (or any boneless white fish fillets), cut into cubes

freshly ground black pepper

2 tablespoons chopped parsley, to garnish

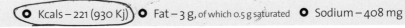

NUTRITIONAL FACTS   ● Kcals – 221 (930 Kj) ● Fat – 3 g, of which 0.5 g saturated ● Sodium – 408 mg

NUTRITIONAL TIPS SERVE 4

There are many good reasons to eat fish. It is delicious and nutritious, quick to cook, easy to prepare and extremely versatile. White fish such as cod, haddock, sea bass, monkfish, plaice, sole, halibut and turbot are all low in

calories, low in fat and saturated fat and high in protein, minerals and vitamins. So, although these fine fish are low in omega-3 fatty acids, they are to be valued just as much as oily fish in bringing variety to your diet and helping you beat heart disease.

orange & cider poached mackerel

Preparation time: 15 minutes
Cooking time: 10 minutes

Serves 4

1 Heat the oil in a large nonstick saucepan, add the pepper, spring onions and ginger and cook, stirring, for 1–2 minutes. Stir in the orange rind, cider, orange and lemon juices and soy sauce. Bring to the boil.

2 Reduce the heat and add the fish. Cover and cook for 5 minutes until the fish starts to flake when tested with a fork. Using a fish slice or slotted spoon, remove the fish from the cooking liquid and place on a plate. Cover with foil. Keep warm in the oven.

3 Add the coriander and pepper to taste to the cooking liquid. Bring to the boil. Boil rapidly until the mixture reduces to a sauce consistency. Serve with Tabbouleh (see page 60) or Baked Beetroot, Spinach & Orange Salad (see page 58), if liked.

1 red pepper, cored, deseeded and
   finely diced
2 spring onions, sliced
2.5–5cm (1–2 inch) piece of
   fresh root ginger, peeled
   and thinly sliced
1 teaspoon olive oil
1 teaspoon grated orange rind
125 ml (4 fl oz) dry cider
125 ml (4 fl oz) orange juice
2 tablespoons lemon juice
1 teaspoon reduced-salt soy sauce
4 mackerel fillets, about 150 g
   (5 oz) each, skinned
2 tablespoons chopped fresh
   coriander
freshly ground black pepper

NUTRITIONAL FACTS ● Kcals – 208 (875 Kj) ● Fat – 4 g, of which 1 g saturated ● Sodium – 144 mg

NUTRITIONAL TIPS
Although mackerel is the best source of omega-3 fatty acids, remember that all fish is good for you and and should be eaten on a regular basis to ensure your diet gets the full benefit. A good tip is to keep a good supply of frozen fish, and frozen food generally, in the freezer. They are just as nutritious as fresh foods in some cases and can act as the perfect healthy eating, convenient way to cook your evening meal.

sea bass with mushroom & mixed herb stuffing

Preparation time: 15 minutes

Cooking time: 40 minutes

Serves 2

1 Heat 1 teaspoon of the oil in a nonstick frying pan and gently cook the mushrooms for about 5 minutes until tender. Season to taste. Remove the pan from the heat and add the lemon rind and juice and herbs.

2 Meanwhile, cook the potatoes in boiling water or a steamer for about 10 minutes until just tender. Drain and allow to cool. Place the potatoes and garlic in a roasting tin, brush with most of the remaining oil and roast in a preheated oven, 200°C (400°F), Gas Mark 6, for about 20 minutes, until golden brown.

3 Make a crisscross incision on the skin side of the fish (to prevent the fish from curling). Make a cut lengthways down the side of each fillet into the centre and fold open creating a pocket for the stuffing. Brush with the remaining oil and stuff with the mushroom and herb mixture. Close up the fish to its original shape.

4 Season with pepper to taste and place on top of the potatoes. Return to the oven and bake for 5–6 minutes (depending on size) until cooked through.

5 Serve with the fish placed on top of the potatoes and garnished with chopped herbs.

1 tablespoon olive oil

125 g (4 oz) mixed mushrooms, preferably wild, sliced

grated rind and juice of 1 lemon

handful of mixed herbs (such as flat leaf parsley, thyme, green or purple basil), roughly chopped

14 tiny new potatoes

1 garlic clove, crushed

2 sea bass fillets, about 125 g (4 oz) each

freshly ground black pepper

chopped herbs, to garnish

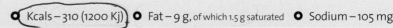

NUTRITIONAL FACTS   Kcals – 310 (1200 Kj)   Fat – 9 g, of which 1.5 g saturated   Sodium – 105 mg

NUTRITIONAL TIPS   *Serve 2*

Sea bass contains a moderate amount of omega-3 fatty acids at 0.4 g per serving (100 g/3½ oz). Our usual average daily intake of EPA and DHA is estimated at only 0.2 g per day, far short of the recommended 1 g per day.

Enjoy spinach with any fish dish. It is a good source of alpha-linolenic acid (see page 18) and you can add a further 0.9 g of omega-3 to your meal. Spinach contains 0.9 g omega-3 fatty acids per 100 g (3½ oz).

creamy kedgeree with peas

Preparation time: 15 minutes

Cooking time: 15 minutes

Serves 4

1 Cook the rice following the instructions on the packet. Place in a warmed serving dish.

2 Meanwhile, poach the fish in the milk in a saucepan for about 5 minutes until just cooked. Strain, reserving the cooking liquid. Skin and flake the fish, removing any stray bones, and set aside.

3 In a separate small saucepan, heat the oil and add the spring onions and curry paste. Cook gently for about 5 minutes until soft.

4 Combine the fish, rice, spring onion mixture, peas and chopped eggs in a large saucepan. Heat through, adding a little of the reserved cooking liquid if necessary. Season to taste with pepper.

5 Serve, garnished with tomatoes, parsley and lemon wedges.

250 g (8 oz) basmati rice

250 g (8 oz) haddock or any white fish

250 g (8 oz) smoked haddock

450 ml (¾ pint) semi-skimmed milk

1 teaspoon olive oil

2 spring onions, chopped

2 teaspoons curry paste

125 g (4 oz) frozen peas, cooked

2 hard-boiled eggs, shelled and chopped

freshly ground black pepper

To Garnish

chopped tomatoes

chopped parsley

lemon wedges

NUTRITIONAL FACTS   ● Kcals – 460 (1932 Kj)   ● Fat – 8 g, of which 2 g saturated   ● Sodium – 672 mg

NUTRITIONAL TIPS Serve 4
Basmati rice has the lowest glycaemic index (GI) of any rice. The GI of rice depends upon its amylose content – a type of starch that is broken down and absorbed relatively slowly by the body.

fisherman's pie with fresh spinach

Preparation time: 15 minutes
Cooking time: 40 minutes

Serves 4

1 In a large saucepan, poach the fish in the milk with the bay leaf for 10 minutes until tender. Strain, retaining the cooking liquid. Skin and flake the fish, removing any stray bones, and set aside.

2 Meanwhile, heat the oil in a small saucepan, add the onion and carrot and cook gently for about 4 minutes. Steam the spinach and squeeze out any excess moisture.

3 Pour the fish cooking liquid into a saucepan. Add the cornflour paste and heat gently, stirring constantly, until thickened. Reduce the heat and simmer for at least 5 minutes. Remove from the heat. Add the mustard and season to taste with pepper.

4 Place the fish, egg quarters and vegetables in an ovenproof dish. Pour over the sauce. Top with the mashed potatoes. Bake in a preheated oven, 180°C (350°F), Gas Mark 4, for 20 minutes.

5 Garnish with tomatoes and return to the oven for 5 minutes. Serve with peas or baked beans, if liked.

500 g (1 lb) white fish, such as a
  mixture of smoked and
  unsmoked cod or haddock
300 ml (½ pint) skimmed milk
1 bay leaf
1 teaspoon olive oil
1 onion, finely chopped
1 carrot, finely chopped
2 large handfuls of spinach leaves
1 tablespoon cornflour, blended
  with a little cold water
1 teaspoon mustard
2 hard-boiled eggs, shelled and
  quartered
500 g (1 lb) cooked potatoes,
  mashed with semi-skimmed milk
  and unsaturated spread
freshly ground black pepper
sliced tomatoes, to garnish

NUTRITIONAL FACTS   ◉ Kcals – 360 (1512 Kj) ◉ Fat – 11 g, of which 2 g saturated ◉ Sodium – 822 mg

NUTRITIONAL TIPS   Serve 4
Baking, steaming, grilling, griddling, microwaving and frying cause little loss of nutrients when cooking fish. Frying fish adds fat, particularly if the fish is battered or crumbed. Poaching fish, as in this recipe, leaches nearly half of the minerals into the cooking water but these are retrieved in the white sauce. This fish pie is crowned with mashed potato rather than pastry, making a huge fat – and saturated fat – saving. Topping any pie with mashed potato rather than pastry is a good way to lower the fat content.

potato & olive bread

Preparation time: 25 minutes, plus proving
Cooking time: 40 minutes

Makes 1 loaf

1 Place the mashed potatoes in a large bowl with the flour. Blend the fresh yeast with the milk. If using dried yeast, dissolve the sugar in the milk, then sprinkle over the yeast and leave in a warm place for about 10 minutes until frothy. Add the yeast mixture and water to the dry ingredients and mix to form a fairly firm dough.

2 Turn on to a floured surface and knead for about 10 minutes until smooth and even. Shape into a ball, place inside an oiled plastic bag and leave in a warm place until doubled in size.

3 Turn out the dough and knead until smooth, adding two-thirds of the olives. Make into a loaf-like shape or shape to fit a greased 1 kg (2 lb) loaf tin. Cover with an oiled plastic bag and leave to prove in a warm place until the dough reaches the top of the tin. Remove the plastic bag and sprinkle with the remaining olives.

4 Bake in a preheated oven, 220°C (425°F), Gas Mark 7, for about 40 minutes, either on a baking sheet if cooking it free-form or in the loaf tin, until the base of the loaf sounds hollow when tapped. Cool on a wire rack.

125 g (4 oz) cooked potatoes, mashed with 1 tablespoon unsaturated spread
500 g (1 lb) strong white plain flour
15 g (½ oz) fresh yeast or 1½ level teaspoons dried yeast plus 1 teaspoon sugar
150 ml (¼ pint) warm milk
150 ml (¼ pint) warm water
15 pitted black olives, thinly sliced

NUTRITIONAL TIPS

Bread can contain a surprising amount of salt, so by making your own you can limit the amount. Salt substitutes are useful but remember that most of them still contain some salt, and that you can make tasty bread without using any salt at all. This unusual bread contains a reasonable amount of salt because there is 70 mg sodium in each black olive. Rinse the olives and dry them thoroughly on kitchen paper before slicing them, to remove some of the salt.

*figures for whole loaf

garlic mash

Preparation time: 10 minutes
Cooking time: 1¼ hours

Serves 4

1 Prick the potatoes with a fork and bake in a preheated oven, 220°C (425°F), Gas Mark 7, for 1–¼ hours until tender.

2 Meanwhile, remove the outer skin from the head of garlic but do not separate the cloves. Slice off the top. Wrap in foil, shiny side inwards. Place on a baking sheet and roast on a lower shelf in the oven for 45 minutes until the garlic flesh is softened to a purée.

3 Holding the baked potato with an oven glove, pierce a cross in the top of each potato with a fork. Squeeze so that the flesh rises up through the skin. Scoop into a bowl and mash with a fork. (Save the crunchy skins for a snack.) Squeeze the roasted garlic flesh into the potatoes and mash thoroughly. Mix in the stock and milk, a tablespoon of each at a time, until the desired texture is achieved. Season to taste with pepper, then stir in the chives (if using).

OR YOU COULD TRY...
CHEESE MASH: Replace the stock and milk with 1–2 tablespoons natural fromage frais or yogurt and 2–3 tablespoons Parmesan cheese.
CELERIAC MASH: Mash potatoes with 375 g (12 oz) peeled, chopped and boiled celeriac. Add skimmed milk, a little unsaturated spread and nutmeg.

1 firm head of garlic

3 baking potatoes, about 300 g (10 oz) each, scrubbed

3–4 tablespoons warm Vegetable Stock (see page 138)

3–4 tablespoons warm skimmed milk

1 tablespoon snipped chives (optional)

freshly ground black pepper

NUTRITIONAL FACTS   ● Kcals – 185 (777 Kj)   ● Fat – less than 1 g, of which a trace saturated   ● Sodium – 24 mg

NUTRITIONAL TIPS
Baked potatoes make the best mashed potatoes – smooth, rich and creamy – and if you follow this recipe they are surprisingly low in fat. The warm roasted garlic is also ideal for spreading straight on to French bread.

lean lasagne

1 For the meat sauce, place the aubergines, onions, garlic, stock and wine in a large nonstick saucepan. Cover and simmer briskly for 5 minutes.

2 Uncover and cook for about 5 minutes until the aubergine is tender and the liquid is absorbed, adding a little more stock if necessary. Remove from the heat, allow to cool slightly, then purée in a food processor or blender.

3 Meanwhile, brown the mince in a nonstick frying pan. Drain off any fat. Add the aubergine mixture, tomatoes and pepper to taste. Simmer briskly, uncovered, for about 10 minutes until thickened.

4 For the cheese sauce, beat the egg whites with the ricotta. Beat in the milk and 4 tablespoons of Parmesan. Season to taste with pepper.

5 To make the lasagne, alternate layers of meat sauce, lasagne and cheese sauce. Start with meat sauce and finish with cheese sauce. Sprinkle with the remaining Parmesan. Bake in a preheated oven, 180°C (350°F), Gas Mark 4, for 30–40 minutes until browned.

200 g (7 oz) pre-cooked sheets of
    lasagne
freshly ground black pepper

MEAT SAUCE

2 aubergines, peeled and diced

2 red onions, chopped

2 garlic cloves, crushed

300 ml (½ pint) Vegetable Stock
    (see page 138)

4 tablespoons red wine

500 g (1 lb) extra-lean mince

2 x 400 g (13 oz) cans chopped
    tomatoes

CHEESE SAUCE

3 egg whites

250 g (8 oz) ricotta cheese

175 ml (6 fl oz) skimmed milk

6 tablespoons freshly grated
    Parmesan cheese

NUTRITIONAL FACTS 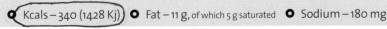 Kcals – 340 (1428 Kj) ⬤ Fat – 11 g, of which 5 g saturated ⬤ Sodium – 180 mg

NUTRITIONAL TIPS

Despite its Mediterranean origins, lasagne can be even higher in fat and calories than fried foods and chips. In this reduced-fat version, the white sauce is made from low-fat ricotta cheese, which tastes sweet and creamy.

macaroni cheese surprise

1 Cook the macaroni according to the packet instructions until just tender and drain.

2 Meanwhile, lightly cook all the vegetables so that they remain crunchy. Drain well.

3 Place the cornflour and a little of the milk in a saucepan. Blend to a smooth paste. Heat gently, adding the rest of the milk and whisking continuously until the sauce boils and thickens. Add three-quarters of the cheese, the mustard and cayenne pepper to taste.

4 Mix together the pasta, vegetables and sauce and spoon into an ovenproof dish. Scatter with the remaining cheese and sprinkle with a little cayenne pepper to garnish. Bake in a preheated oven, 200°C (400°F), Gas Mark 6, for about 25 minutes, until golden brown.

Or you could try...

Any vegetables could be lightly cooked and added to the cheesy mixture, such as peas, sweetcorn, mixed peppers, carrots, mushrooms and mixed vegetables.

175 g (6 oz) wholemeal macaroni

2 carrots, cut into small, chunky batons

250 g (8 oz) broccoli florets

1 large leek, trimmed and thickly sliced

50 g (2 oz) cornflour

600 ml (1 pint) skimmed milk

100 g (3½ oz) low-fat mature hard cheese, grated

1 teaspoon mustard

pinch of cayenne pepper, plus extra to garnish

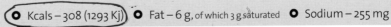

NUTRITIONAL FACTS   Kcals – 308 (1293 Kj)   ○ Fat – 6 g, of which 3 g saturated   ○ Sodium – 255 mg

NUTRITIONAL TIPS   Serve 4

All pasta is naturally healthy – rich in carbohydrates and low in fat. Wholemeal pasta is made from the whole grain and contains more insoluble fibre than the white variety, which helps to prevent constipation and other bowel problems.

The 'surprise' in this all-time family favourite is the addition of vegetables – an easy and delicious way of including an extra portion so that you go some way to eating your five portions of fruit and vegetables a day.

farfalle with anchovy & oregano sauce

Preparation time: 10 minutes

Cooking time: 15 minutes

Serves 4

1 Heat the oil in a small saucepan, add the garlic and fry gently for about 5 minutes until golden.

2 Reduce the heat to very low, stir in the anchovies and cook very gently for about 10 minutes until they have completely disintegrated.

3 Meanwhile, cook the pasta according to the packet instructions until just tender.

4 Stir the oregano and pepper to taste into the sauce.

5 Drain the pasta and turn into a warmed serving dish. Pour over the sauce, sprinkle with the parsley and gently toss together. Serve with Parmesan cheese and a crisp Mediterranean salad, if liked.

1 tablespoon olive oil

2 garlic cloves, finely chopped

50 g (2 oz) canned anchovy fillets, drained

375 g (12 oz) dried farfalle

2 teaspoons oregano, finely chopped

3 tablespoons chopped parsley

freshly ground black pepper

grated Parmesan cheese, to serve

NUTRITIONAL FACTS 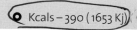 Kcals – 390 (1653 Kj) Fat – 7 g, of which less than 1 g saturated Sodium – 500 mg

NUTRITIONAL TIPS SERVE

All pasta has a very low glycaemic index (GI). This is because it is made from high-protein semolina (finely cracked wheat) and has a dense food matrix that resists disruption in the small intestine. But even pasta made from fine flour instead of semolina has a relatively low GI. Interestingly, there is some evidence that thicker pasta has a lower GI than thin varieties. The addition of egg to fresh pasta lowers the GI by increasing the protein content. A higher protein level slows the stomach in emptying.

wild rice jambalaya

1 Place the wild rice in a saucepan with water to cover. Bring to the boil and boil for 5 minutes. Remove the pan from heat and cover tightly. Leave to steam for about 10 minutes until the grains are tender. Drain.

2 Heat the oil in a large nonstick frying pan. Add the celery, peppers, onion, bacon and garlic. Cook, stirring, for 3–4 minutes until the vegetables are soft. Stir in the tomato purée and thyme. Cook for another 2 minutes.

3 Add the wild rice, long-grain rice, chilli, cayenne pepper, pimientos (if using), tomatoes, stock and wine. Bring to the boil. Reduce the heat and simmer for 10 minutes until the rice is tender but still firm to the bite.

4 Add the prawns or mycoprotein and cook, stirring occasionally, for 5 minutes, until the prawns have turned opaque. Spoon into large warmed bowls. Scatter with coriander or parsley and serve. Accompany with crusty bread, if liked.

125 g (4 oz) wild rice

1 teaspoon olive oil

50 g (2 oz) celery, chopped

½ red pepper, cored, deseeded and
  diced

½ green or yellow pepper, cored,
  deseeded and diced

1 onion, chopped

1 rindless lean back bacon rasher,
  trimmed of fat

2 garlic cloves, crushed

2 tablespoons tomato purée

1 tablespoon chopped thyme

125 g (4 oz) long-grain rice

1 green chilli, deseeded and finely
  chopped

½ teaspoon cayenne pepper

1 tablespoon chopped canned
  pimientos (optional)

400 g (13 oz) can tomatoes, drained

300 ml (½ pint) Chicken Stock
  (see page 138)

150 ml (¼ pint) dry white wine

250 g (8 oz) raw medium prawns
  or mycoprotein pieces

3 tablespoons chopped fresh
  coriander or parsley, to garnish

NUTRITIONAL FACTS ⊙ Kcals – 370 (1554 Kj) ⊙ Fat – 3 g, of which less than 1 g saturated ⊙ Sodium – 680 mg

NUTRITIONAL TIPS   SERVE 4

Prawns and other shellfish are generally low in fat and
contain a small amount of omega-3 fatty acids. However,
they contain a reasonable amount of cholesterol, but little
appears to be absorbed by the body.

chicken, wild mushroom & fennel rice

Preparation time: 10 minutes
Cooking time: 30 minutes

Serves 4

1 Heat the oil in a saucepan and gently fry the fennel, onion and garlic for 5 minutes. Add the mushrooms and cook for 2 minutes. Stir in the rice and gently fry for 2 minutes. Add the wine and stir until absorbed by the rice.

2 Add half the stock and bring to the boil, then lower the heat and simmer gently, stirring frequently, until absorbed. Add the rest of the stock a little at a time, allowing each amount to be absorbed before adding the next.

3 After about 15 minutes, add the chicken, dill and lemon rind and juice. Cook for about 5 minutes more, until the rice is creamy but still firm to the bite. Season to taste with pepper and turn into a warmed serving dish Sprinkle with pine nuts and garnish with dill sprigs.

1 tablespoon olive oil

1 fennel bulb, trimmed and finely
    sliced

1 onion, finely sliced

1 garlic clove, crushed

175 g (6 oz) mixed mushrooms,
    including some wild, sliced

250 g (8 oz) basmati rice

150 ml (¼ pint) dry white wine

450 ml (¾ pint) Chicken Stock
    (see page 138)

250 g (8 oz) cooked chicken, diced

½ bunch of dill, finely chopped,
finely grated rind and juice of
    1 lemon

freshly ground black pepper

25 g (1 oz) pine nuts, toasted

dill sprigs, to garnish

NUTRITIONAL FACTS   ● Kcals – 440 (1848 Kj)   ● Fat – 10 g, of which 1 g saturated   ● Sodium – 260 mg

NUTRITIONAL TIPS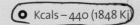
Traditional Asian-style diets, characterized by relatively large quantities of rice and small quantities of meat, offer many heart-health benefits. Paella mirrors this principle and can be made with a variety of ingredients such as

vegetables, fish and meat. Rice varies markedly in its glycaemic index (GI) depending on the variety. Many types of rice consumed in Great Britain have a high GI, while basmati rice from India and the rice eaten in Japan both have a low GI.

red kidney bean & aubergine pilaf

Preparation time: 15 minutes

Cooking time: 40 minutes

Serves 4

1 Place the water in a large saucepan and bring to the boil. Add the rice and turmeric and stir well to prevent the rice from sticking. Cover and simmer for 30 minutes without stirring. Remove from the heat.

2 Meanwhile, heat the oil in a nonstick frying pan, add the onion, garlic, celery, pepper and aubergine and cook gently for 3 minutes without browning. Add the tomatoes and mushrooms, stir well and cook for 3–4 minutes.

3 Stir the beans and the vegetable mixture into the rice, cover and cook very gently for 10 minutes.

4 Remove from the heat and leave for 5 minutes. Season to taste with pepper and stir in the parsley. Transfer to a warmed serving dish to serve.

Or you could try...

This dish is also delicious with the addition of two 275 g (9 oz) cooked and chopped boneless, skinless chicken joints before the tomatoes and mushrooms, for an alternative non-vegetarian supper.

450 ml (¾ pint) water

250 g (8 oz) brown long-grain rice

½ teaspoon turmeric

1 tablespoon vegetable oil

1 large onion, finely chopped

1 garlic clove, finely chopped

1 celery stick, chopped

1 green pepper, cored, deseeded and chopped

1 aubergine, diced

2 tomatoes, skinned and chopped

125 g (4 oz) mushrooms, sliced

200 g (7 oz) canned kidney beans, rinsed and drained

2 tablespoons chopped parsley

freshly ground black pepper

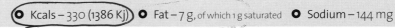

NUTRITIONAL FACTS   Kcals – 330 (1386 Kj)   Fat – 7 g, of which 1 g saturated   Sodium – 144 mg

NUTRITIONAL TIPS   SERVE 4

Beans are a good source of protein, especially when they are served with a cereal food such as rice, bread or pasta. They are low in fat, high in fibre and rich in many nutrients, providing iron, zinc, calcium, folate and soluble fibre.

tomato & herb pizza pie

Preparation time: 15 minutes
Cooking time: 35–40 minutes

Serves 6

1 For the scone base, sieve the flour into a mixing bowl and rub in the spread until the mixture resembles fine breadcrumbs. Add just enough milk to form a soft dough. Turn out on to a lightly floured surface and knead until smooth. Roll out to a 23–25 cm (9–10 inches) diameter round, then place on a greased baking sheet.

2 For the topping, heat the oil in a large saucepan, add the onion and garlic and fry gently for 5 minutes until softened. Add the pepper, tomatoes, tomato purée and basil or thyme and simmer, uncovered, for about 10 minutes until the mixture is thick. Season with pepper.

3 Spread the tomato mixture over the base to the edge. Top with the cheese. Bake in the centre of a preheated oven, 220°C (425°F), Gas Mark 7, for 20–25 minutes until the topping is bubbling. Garnish with basil sprigs before serving.

OR YOU COULD TRY...

- Anchovy fillets and black olives
- Red onion, feta cheese, red pepper and rocket
- Spinach and ricotta
- Caponata Ratatouille (see page 66)

BASE

300 g (10 oz) wholemeal self-raising flour
50 g (2 oz) unsaturated spread
150 ml (¼ pint) skimmed milk

TOPPING

1 tablespoon olive oil
2 large onions, chopped
1–2 garlic cloves
1 green or red pepper, cored, deseeded and sliced
2 x 400 g (13 oz) cans tomatoes
2 tablespoons tomato purée
large handful of basil or thyme, chopped
125 g (4 oz) low-fat mozzarella cheese, sliced
freshly ground black pepper
basil sprigs, to garnish

NUTRITIONAL FACTS   ● Kcals – 340 (1428 Kj)   ● Fat – 15g, of which 5 g saturated   ● Sodium – 268 mg

NUTRITIONAL TIPS   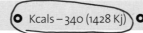 SERVE 6
Home-made pizzas can be very healthy, with a starchy base topped with your own choice of fresh vegetables and low-fat ingredients. Look out for half-fat mozzarella, which has only 10 g of fat per 100 g (3½ oz).

Pizzas are fun to make and will encourage children to take an interest in food, cooking and their health. Before buying pizzas, check the label and choose those with the least fat – you will be surprised at how much the fat content can vary.

thai sesame & tofu stir-fry

Preparation time: 15 minutes
Cooking time: 10 minutes

 Serves 4

1 In a small bowl, mix together the sesame oil and 1 tablespoon teriyaki sauce. Brush over both sides of the tofu. Sprinkle one side of each piece of tofu with half the sesame seeds. Mix together the remaining teriyaki sauce, vinegar or sherry and soy sauce. Set aside.

2 Heat a large wok or frying pan. Brush with a little of the groundnut oil. Add the tofu, seed side down, and cook for 2 minutes. Sprinkle the remaining sesame seeds over the tofu. Turn over and cook for 2 minutes more until crisp. Remove the tofu from the pan and keep warm.

3 Brush the pan with a little more groundnut oil, then add the mangetouts, carrot, bean sprouts and spring onion batons. Stir-fry for 2–3 minutes until tender yet still crisp. Add the reserved teriyaki sauce mixture. Stir-fry for 1 minute.

4 Divide the hot noodles between warmed serving bowls. Add the watercress, spoon over the vegetables and top with the tofu. Garnish with the shredded spring onion. Serve with a green salad, if liked.

1 teaspoon sesame oil

2 tablespoons Teriyaki Sauce (see page 140), or ready-prepared

400 g (13 oz) firm tofu, cut into 4 thick slices

2 tablespoons sesame seeds

1 tablespoon rice wine vinegar or sherry

2 teaspoons reduced-salt soy sauce

1 tablespoon groundnut oil

16 mangetouts

1 carrot, cut into thin strips

125 g (4 oz) bean sprouts

2 spring onions, white parts cut into 5 cm (2 inch) batons, green tops shredded for garnish

250 g (8 oz) rice noodles, prepared according to the packet instructions

50 g (2 oz) watercress, broken into sprigs

lentil & vegetable khichiri

Preparation time: 10 minutes, plus soaking
Cooking time: 35 minutes

Serves 4

1 Wash the lentils and rice together, then soak in a bowl of water for 15–20 minutes. Drain and set aside.

2 Heat the oil in a saucepan, add the onion, cinnamon, cloves, cardamom (if using) and cumin seeds and fry gently for about 5 minutes, stirring frequently, until the onion turns a deep golden colour.

3 Add the turmeric, chilli powder, ginger and garlic paste, yogurt and a little water and cook for 2–3 minutes, adding a little more water if necessary. Stir in the beans, carrot and tomato and cook for 1–2 minutes.

4 Add the rice and lentils, stir to mix, then add the measured water. Cover the pan with a close-fitting lid and bring to the boil. Reduce the heat and simmer for 20 minutes, then allow to stand for 3–4 minutes before serving.

50 g (2 oz) red lentils

200 g (7 oz) basmati or long-grain rice

2 tablespoons vegetable oil

1 onion, finely chopped

1 cm (½ inch) piece of cinnamon stick

1 black cardamom pod, split or bruised (optional)

1 teaspoon cumin seeds

2–3 cloves

¼ teaspoon turmeric

½ teaspoon chilli powder

2 teaspoons Ginger and Garlic Paste (see page 140)

1 tablespoon natural yogurt

75 g (3 oz) green beans, chopped

75 g (3 oz) carrot, diced

50 g (2 oz) tomato, chopped

450 ml (¾ pint) water

NUTRITIONAL FACTS Kcals – 300 (1260 Kj) Fat – 8 g, of which 1 g saturated Sodium – 26 mg

NUTRITIONAL TIPS
Pulses including lentils, chickpeas, soya beans and kidney beans are an important part of a low glycaemic index (GI) diet. Asian and Mediterranean populations eat approximately 250 g (8 oz) or more of pulses per week,

and therefore it is recommended that you try to eat beans – either dried or canned – at least twice a week. There is a very wide range to choose from and they make a tasty and satisfying addition to soups, casseroles, stews, salads and sauces.

aubergine & potato soya moussaka

| Preparation time: 45 minutes
 Cooking time: 45 minutes | | **Serves 4** |

1 Heat most of the oil in a nonstick frying pan and fry the aubergines in batches for about 10 minutes until lightly browned. Set aside. Repeat with the potato slices, carefully adding a little boiling water or stock if necessary. Set aside with the aubergine.

2 Add the onion to the pan and cook for 5 minutes. Add the soya mince and cook for 5 minutes. Add the wine, stock, passata, tomato purée, spices, thyme and pepper to taste. Gently simmer, uncovered, for about 15 minutes until thickened. Remove from the heat.

3 For the topping, blend the cornflour with a little of the milk. Place in a saucepan over a low heat and gradually whisk in the remaining milk. Continue stirring until the sauce thickens. Simmer for 2–3 minutes. Stir in the nutmeg and allow to cool before whisking in the egg.

4 Brush an ovenproof dish with the remaining oil. Place a layer of potato in the bottom, cover with a layer of the sauce, followed by a layer of aubergines. Continue layering in this order. Pour the topping over the dish and sprinkle with Parmesan. Bake in a preheated oven, 190°C (375°F), Gas Mark 5, for about 45 minutes until browned.

1 tablespoon olive oil

2 medium aubergines, thinly sliced

2 large potatoes, thinly sliced

1 large onion, chopped

150 g (5 oz) dried soya mince, prepared according to packet instructions

300 ml (½ pint) red wine

300 ml (½ pint) Vegetable Stock (see page 138)

300 ml (½ pint) passata

2 tablespoons tomato purée

½ teaspoon ground cinnamon

¼ teaspoon ground nutmeg

½ teaspoon dried thyme

freshly ground black pepper

25 g (1 oz) cornflour

450 ml (¾ pint) skimmed milk

¼ teaspoon ground nutmeg

1 egg

50 g (2 oz) Parmesan cheese, grated

NUTRITIONAL FACTS   **O** Kcals – 445 (2226 Kj)   **O** Fat – 12g, of which 4 g saturated   **O** Sodium – 1932 mg

NUTRITIONAL TIPS   SERVE 4
To reduce the amount of oil used in frying vegetables, add a little hot stock or wine or sherry so that they sauté or steam in their own juices. A serving of this moussaka gives 18 g of soya protein and if eaten regularly you could expect a total cholesterol and LDL cholesterol lowering effect of 7 per cent.

sweet potato & cannellini falafel

Preparation time: 20 minutes
Cooking time: 10 minutes

Serves 6

1 Boil or microwave the sweet potato until tender, then drain. Place in a bowl and mash. Set aside.

2 Heat the oil in a nonstick frying pan, add the garlic, cumin and ground coriander. Cook, stirring, for 1–2 minutes until fragrant. Stir in the tomato purée. Cook for 3–4 minutes until the mixture becomes deep red and develops a rich aroma. Stir in the beans or chickpeas.

3 Place the fresh coriander, tahini and lemon juice in a food processor or blender and process to form a coarse paste.

4 Mix the bean mixture and breadcrumbs with the sweet potato. Shape the mixture into 2.5 cm (1 inch) round patties. If the mixture feels too wet to shape into patties you may need to add some extra breadcrumbs. Roll in flour to coat. Place on a plate lined with clingfilm. Cover and refrigerate until ready to cook – the patties can be made up to 1 day in advance.

5 Grill the falafel under a preheated hot grill for 3–4 minutes each side until golden and crispy.

6 Spread the bread with hummus. Top with lettuce, tabbouleh and onion. Place 3 falafel in each pitta and flatten slightly. Sprinkle with lemon juice to taste and serve immediately.

6 pitta breads, warmed

1 tablespoon low-fat hummus or Tahini Hummus (see page 45)

100 g (3½ oz) shredded lettuce

175 g Tabbouleh (see page 60)

1 red onion, thinly sliced

lemon juice, to serve

Falafel

400 g (13 oz) orange sweet potato, cut into chunks

2 teaspoons olive oil

1 clove garlic, crushed

2 teaspoons ground cumin

1 teaspoon ground coriander

1 tablespoon tomato purée

400 g (13 oz) can cannellini beans, rinsed and drained

2 tablespoons chopped fresh coriander

1 tablespoon tahini (sesame seed paste)

1 tablespoon lemon juice

75 g (3 oz) dry breadcrumbs

flour, for coating

NUTRITIONAL FACTS *   ○ Kcals – 215 (903Kj)   ○ Fat – 8 g, of which 1 g saturated   ○ Sodium – 245 mg

NUTRITIONAL TIPS   *SERVE 6*

Sweet potatoes are full of antioxidants, particularly the ACE
vitamins and beta-carotene. Like yams and new potatoes,
they are digested more slowly than all other potatoes and
help to lower the overall glycaemic index (GI) of the diet.

* figures per serving of felafel only

thai beef & mixed pepper stir-fry

Preparation time: 20 minutes
Cooking time: 10 minutes

Serves 4

1 Cut the beef into long, thin strips, cutting across the grain.

2 Heat the oil in a wok or large frying pan over a high heat. Add the garlic and stir-fry for 1 minute.

3 Add the beef and stir-fry for 2–3 minutes until lightly coloured. Stir in the lemon grass and ginger and remove the pan from the heat. Remove the beef from the pan and set side

4 Add the peppers and onion and stir-fry for 2–3 minutes until the onions are just turning golden brown and are slightly softened.

5 Return the beef to the pan, stir in the lime juice and season to taste with pepper. Serve with boiled noodles or rice, if liked.

500 g (1 lb) lean beef fillet

1 tablespoon sesame oil

1 garlic clove, finely chopped

1 lemon grass stalk, finely shredded

2.5 cm (1 inch) piece of fresh root ginger, peeled and finely chopped

1 red pepper, cored, deseeded and thickly sliced

1 green pepper, cored, deseeded and thickly sliced

1 onion, thickly sliced

2 tablespoons lime juice

freshly ground black pepper

NUTRITIONAL FACTS * ● Kcals – 255 (1067 Kj) ● Fat – 12 g, of which 3 g saturated ● Sodium – 4 mg

NUTRITIONAL TIPS *SERVE 4*
Stir-frying is a healthy and easy way to cook. It is important to measure the oil by the teaspoon or tablespoon and use the minimum amount necessary. You can stir-fry in water, stock or wine to reduce the fat content further.

* figures per serving without noodles or rice

cranberry & orange turkey fillets

Preparation time: 5 minutes
Cooking time: 45–50 minutes

Serves 4

1 In a small bowl, mix together the honey, orange juice and rind, allspice and cranberries.

2 Remove all visible fat from the turkey breasts. Place in an ovenproof dish and pour half the cranberry mixture over the turkey. Bake in a preheated oven, 190°C (375°F), Gas Mark 5, for 15 minutes.

3 Remove the dish from the oven, turn the turkey pieces and pour over the remaining sauce. Return to the oven for a further 30–35 minutes. Serve with Spiced Roast Roots (see page 68) or baked potatoes and green leafy vegetables, if liked.

2 teaspoons honey

300 ml (½ pint) orange juice

1 teaspoon grated orange rind

½ teaspoon ground allspice

500 g (1 lb) cranberries (fresh, canned or frozen and thawed)

4 boneless, skinless turkey breast fillets, about 125 g (4 oz) each

NUTRITIONAL FACTS   Kcals – 330 (1386 Kj)   Fat – 2 g, of which less than 1 g saturated   Sodium – 120 mg

NUTRITIONAL TIPS 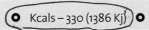
Even when cooking lean meat such as poultry be sure to remove the fat-laden skin and trim away all the visible fat. The white meat contains less fat than the dark meat, but avoid overcooking the white meat, since it tends to dry out.

Keep moist by basting with stock and wine. Chicken and turkey can easily be substituted for other lean meats in many recipes, such as rabbit, venison and ostrich.

chicken enchiladas with mango salsa

Preparation time: 20 minutes
Cooking time: 25 minutes

Serves 6

1 Heat the oil in a saucepan, add the onion and cook for about 5 minutes until softened. Stir in the beans, chicken, chillies, oregano and fresh tomato. Heat through, then remove from the heat.

2 Place the chilli powder, cumin and blended tomatoes or passata in a saucepan and simmer for 2 minutes. Remove from the heat.

3 Dip each tortilla into the tomato mixture and set aside on a plate. Fill each tortilla with 3 tablespoons of the chicken mixture. Roll up and place seam-side down in an ovenproof dish. Pour two thirds of the mango salsa over the enchiladas. Sprinkle with the cheese and serve with the remaining salsa.

4 Bake in a preheated oven, 180°C (350°F), Gas Mark 4, for about 20 minutes. Place 2 enchilladas on each plate and serve.

2 teaspoons vegetable oil

1 large onion, chopped

250 g (8 oz) canned pinto beans, rinsed and drained

300 g (10 oz) cooked chicken breast, skinned and cubed

4 green chillies, deseeded and chopped

1 teaspoon dried oregano

1 large tomato, chopped

¼ teaspoon chilli powder

¼ teaspoon ground cumin

400 g (13 oz) can tomatoes, blended in a food processor or blender and sieved, or passata

12 corn tortillas

quantity of Mango Salsa (see page 141)

75 g (3 oz) grated low-fat mozzarella cheese

NUTRITIONAL FACTS * ● Kcals – 240 (1048 Kj) ● Fat – 3 g, of which less than 1 g saturated ● Sodium – 190mg

NUTRITIONAL TIPS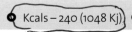
Mexican food has a number of high-fat traps, but it also offers many healthy and delicious dishes. If chosen carefully, and with some minor adjustments, you can enjoy this rich and flavourful cuisine. Enchiladas can be one of the traps because of the high cheese content. In this version, a small amount of reduced-fat cheese is used and the corn tortillas are packed with plenty of high-fibre beans instead.

* figures per enchilada

tandoori chicken

1 Mix together all the ingredients for the marinade in a bowl.

2 Place the chicken in a non-metallic dish. Spoon over the marinade and rub well into the chicken. Cover and refrigerate for 2–4 hours.

3 Scrape the excess marinade from the chicken. Place the chicken on a wire rack set in a roasting tray. Pour in wine or water to the depth of 2.5 cm (1 inch) and add the herb sprigs, to keep the meat moist during cooking.

4 Bake the chicken in a preheated oven, 240°C (475°F), Gas Mark 9, for 10 minutes. Turn over and bake for a further 10 minutes until cooked through. Serve with Herbed Yogurt and Cucumber Sauce (see page 140), and accompany with naan bread, basmati rice and a green salad, if liked.

4 boneless, skinless chicken breasts, about 150 g (5 oz) each
wine or water
a few herb sprigs, such as rosemary, thyme or parsley

MARINADE

1 tablespoon grated fresh root ginger
2 teaspoons coriander seeds, toasted
2 teaspoons rosemary leaves
1 teaspoon grated lemon rind
½ teaspoon ground cardamom
½ teaspoon ground cumin
¼ teaspoon crushed black peppercorns
¼ teaspoon chilli sauce or powder
125 g (4 oz) natural yogurt
1 tablespoon lemon juice

NUTRITIONAL FACTS   ● Kcals – 212 (890 Kj)   ● Fat – 4 g, of which 1 g saturated   ● Sodium – 110 mg

NUTRITIONAL TIPS
Tandoori cooking is traditionally carried out in a very hot clay oven. The food is cooked quickly and the finished product is often slightly charred. The tandoori marinade and cooking method involves no added fat or sugar and

can be used for whole fish, lamb or fish fillets – just adjust the cooking times as necessary. Fish can be cooked on a grill or griddle for 3 minutes each side.

turkish lamb & potato stew

Preparation time: 20 minutes

Cooking time: 2 hours

Serves 6

1 Heat the oil in a large, heavy-based saucepan. Add the lamb and fry, stirring, until sealed and browned all over.

2 Add the onions and garlic and fry gently for about 5 minutes until softened. Add the potatoes, tomatoes, pepper, stock or water and vinegar and bring to the boil. Add the herbs and season well with pepper. Cover and simmer gently for 1 hour.

3 Stir well, then add the aubergine and/or fennel and olives. Bring back to the boil, cover and simmer gently for 45–60 minutes until the lamb is very tender, stirring occasionally. Discard the bay leaves before serving. Serve with pitta bread and a mixed salad, if liked.

1 tablespoon vegetable oil

500 g (1 lb) lean lamb, cut into
  1.5 cm (¾ inch) cubes

4 onions, cut into wedges

2 garlic cloves, crushed

750 g (1½ lb) potatoes, cut into
  chunks

375 g (12 oz) tomatoes, skinned and
  sliced or quartered

1 red or green pepper, cored,
  deseeded and sliced

900 ml (1½ pints) stock or water

2 tablespoons wine vinegar

2 bay leaves

1 teaspoon chopped sage

1 tablespoon chopped dill or fennel

1 aubergine and/or 1 chopped
  fennel bulb

12 pitted black olives

freshly ground black pepper

NUTRITIONAL FACTS 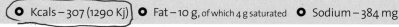 Kcals – 307 (1290 Kj) • Fat – 10 g, of which 4 g saturated • Sodium – 384 mg

NUTRITIONAL TIPS 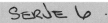 SERVE 6 .
Red meat is commonly regarded as beef, pork and lamb and all can be part of a healthy heart diet providing the meat is extremely lean. Many butchers and supermarkets provide fully trimmed raw meat, but always check the labels (see pages 30–31) on packs of meat. Casseroles and stews can be cooked in advance, cooled and any fat skimmed from the surface to ensure that the dish is very low in fat. Only eat small amounts of the best, leanest meat and surround with plenty of vegetables, beans and starchy carbohydrate foods such as potatoes, pasta, rice and bread.

kofta curry

1 For the koftas, place the onion, ginger, garlic and coriander in a food processor or blender. Process until blended. Place the mince in a bowl and add the blended mixture, spices and cornflour. Knead to mix. Cover and refrigerate for 10–15 minutes, to allow the spices to infuse.

2 For the sauce, heat the oil in a heavy-based saucepan, add the onion and fry gently for 5 minutes. Add the cumin and cardamoms and cook for about 2 minutes until the onions are browned, then add the garlic and ginger paste and remaining spices. Cook, adding a little water when necessary, for about 5 minutes, until the spices darken. Add the tomatoes and yogurt, stirring continuously.

3 Meanwhile, divide the kofta mixture into 16 equal portions and roll each portion into a smooth round ball. Grill the koftas under a preheated medium grill for 10 minutes, turning once to drain off all the excess fat.

4 Add the koftas to the sauce mixture. Cook, stirring, for about 2 minutes, then add the water, cover and simmer for 20–25 minutes. Stir in the chilli and coriander, adding a little boiling water if necessary. Serve with basmati rice and Mushroom and Pea Bhaji (see page 66) if liked.

1 small onion, chopped

2 teaspoons grated fresh root ginger

3 garlic cloves, roughly chopped

3 tablespoons fresh coriander leaves

325 g (11 oz) lean lamb or beef mince

½ teaspoon chilli powder

¼ teaspoon Garam Masala

1 tablespoon cornflour

Sauce

1 tablespoon vegetable oil

1 small onion, finely chopped

¼ teaspoon cumin seeds

2–3 green cardamom pods

2 teaspoons Ginger and Garlic Paste
  (see page 140)

½ teaspoon chilli powder

¼ teaspoon turmeric

¼ teaspoon Garam Masala

75 g (3 oz) tomatoes, chopped

1 tablespoon natural yogurt

450 ml (¾ pint) water

1 green chilli, deseeded and finely
  chopped

2 tablespoons fresh coriander leaves

NUTRITIONAL TIPS   SERVE 4

Indian cuisine is full of heart-healthy ingredients: beans and rice, wholemeal flour, natural yogurt, garlic, ginger, fresh fruit and vegetables, fish, lean meat or no meat at all. The fat-trap is in the preparation with a liberal use of oil.

However, delicious curries can be made with as little as 1 tablespoon of oil, cooking spices and onions gently over a low heat and stirring from time to time. A good curry starts with the leanest meat and the freshest vegetables, so ensure that you go easy on the oil for a healthy curry.

bread & spread pudding

Preparation time: 30 minutes
Cooking time: 45 minutes

 Serves 4

1 Grease a 600 ml (1 pint) pie or ovenproof dish. Cut the bread into triangles and place a layer in the bottom of the dish. Sprinkle with some of the dried fruit and a little grated orange rind. Continue with these layers, finishing with a layer of bread and spread.

2 In a small saucepan, heat the milk with the sugar until it just reaches boiling point, then allow it to cool a little. Add the orange liqueur.

3 Pour the milk mixture over the eggs in a heatproof bowl, whisking to combine. Pour the mixture over the layers of bread and let it soak for about 15 minutes.

4 Sprinkle a little sugar over the top and bake in a preheated oven, 160°C (325°F), Gas Mark 3, for 45 minutes until the top is puffed up and golden.

a little unsaturated spread, for greasing

5 slices wholemeal bread, crusts removed and thinly covered with unsaturated spread

50 g (2 oz) seedless raisins or mixed dried fruit

grated rind of ½ orange

600 ml (1 pint) skimmed milk or vanilla soya milk

25 g (1 oz) sugar, plus extra for sprinkling

splash of Cointreau or Grand Marnier

2 eggs, beaten

NUTRITIONAL FACTS   ○ Kcals – 300 (1260 Kj)   ○ Fat – 10 g, of which 2 g saturated   ○ Sodium – 418 mg

NUTRITIONAL TIPS
Boosting soya intake could have a major effect on reducing the incidence of heart disease. Soya milk is made from ground, whole soya beans. It is lactose- and casein-free and some brands are fortified with calcium, vitamin D and vitamin B12. If you use soya milk in this pudding, you will gain 5 g of soya protein, which translates into a 2 per cent reduction in total and LDL cholesterol. Every little helps!

plum charlotte

Preparation time: 20 minutes
Cooking time: 40–45 minutes

Serves 6

1 Grease the base and sides of a shallow baking dish with a little of the unsaturated spread. Cover the base with some of the breadcrumbs.

2 Place a layer of plums in the dish, sprinkle with some of the sugar and a little lemon rind and juice. Dot with more spread.

3 Continue with these layers until all the ingredients are used up, finishing with a layer of breadcrumbs and dotting with spread.

4 Pour over the orange juice and bake in a preheated oven, 190°C (375°F), Gas Mark 5, for 40–45 minutes until the top is golden brown and the plums are tender.

5 Serve straight from the baking dish. Serve with low-fat custard or natural fromage frais or yogurt, if liked.

50 g (2 oz) unsaturated spread

175 g (6 oz) fresh white
breadcrumbs

750 g (1½ lb) ripe plums, halved and
stoned

100 g (3½ oz) soft brown sugar

finely grated rind and juice of
½ lemon

250 ml (8 fl oz) fresh orange juice

NUTRITIONAL FACTS ○ Kcals – 255 (1071 Kj) ○ Fat – 8 g, of which 2 g saturated ○ Sodium – 220 mg

NUTRITIONAL TIPS
Plums are an ideal fruit to use for a charlotte since they become soft and juicy when they are baked and so blend into the bread. Temperate fruits such as apples and stoned fruit such as plums, peaches, nectarines, grapes and citrus fruits have a lower glycaemic index (GI) than tropical fruits such as mango and pineapple. This means that plums are a good choice for helping to keep the whole glycaemic index of the diet relatively low.

apple & fig crumble

1 Sift the flour in a large bowl and lightly rub in the unsaturated spread until the mixture forms coarse crumbs. Stir in the sugar.

2 Place the fruit into a 1.2 litre (2 pint) ovenproof dish. Add the lemon rind and juice and cinnamon. Spoon the crumble mixture over the fruit and bake in a preheated oven, 180°C (350°F), Gas Mark 4, for 25–30 minutes until golden brown. Serve warm.

OR YOU COULD TRY...

Always remember to use plenty of fruit – 500–750 g (1–1½ lb) – and sweeten slightly sour fruit by mixing with sweeter fruit, a little grated rind and juice of an orange or a variety of dried fruit. Try the following combinations:

- Plum and blackberry
- Rhubarb and strawberry
- Cranberry and apple
- Pear and blackcurrant
- Apricot and peach

125 g (4 oz) wholemeal plain flour

50 g (2 oz) brown sugar

50 g (2 oz) unsaturated spread

500 g (1 lb) cooking apples (such as Bramleys), peeled, cored and sliced

6 dried or fresh figs, diced

grated rind and juice of 1 lemon

1 teaspoon ground cinnamon

NUTRITIONAL FACTS   ● Kcals – 250 (1050 Kj)   ● Fat – 8 g, of which 1.5 g saturated   ● Sodium – 75 mg

NUTRITIONAL TIPS
Figs are high in dietary fibre, low in fat and offer a non-dairy source of calcium, iron and magnesium. They are ideal ingredients in baking, salads and snacks.

strawberry & fromage frais roulade

Preparation time: 30 minutes

Cooking time: 8 minutes

Serves 8

1 Lightly grease a 33 x 23 cm (13 x 9 inch) Swiss roll tin. Line with a single sheet of greaseproof paper to come about 1 cm (½ inch) above the sides of the tin. Lightly grease the paper.

2 In a large bowl, whisk the eggs and sugar over a saucepan of hot water until pale and thick. Sieve the flour and fold into the egg mixture with the hot water. Pour into the prepared tin and bake in a preheated oven, 220°C (425°F), Gas Mark 7, for 8 minutes until golden and set.

3 Meanwhile, place a sheet of greaseproof paper 2.5 cm (1 inch) larger all round than the Swiss roll tin on a clean damp tea towel. Once cooked, turn out the Swiss roll immediately face down on to the greaseproof. Carefully peel off the lining paper. Roll the sponge up tightly with the new greaseproof paper inside. Wrap the tea towel around the outside and place on a wire tray until cool, then unroll carefully.

4 Add half the strawberries to the fromage frais or yogurt and spread over the sponge. Roll the sponge up again and trim the ends. Dust with icing sugar and decorate with a few strawberries. Purée the remaining strawberries in a food processor or blender and serve as a sauce with the roll.

a little unsaturated spread, for greasing

3 eggs

125 g (4 oz) caster sugar

125 g (4 oz) plain flour

1 tablespoon hot water

500 g (1 lb) fresh or frozen, thawed and drained strawberries, or 425 g (14 oz) can strawberries in natural juice, drained

200 g (7 oz) natural fromage frais or yogurt

icing sugar, for dusting

NUTRITIONAL FACTS   ● Kcals – 110 (462 Kj)   ● Fat – 3 g, of which 0.7 g saturated   ● Sodium – 34 mg

NUTRITIONAL TIPS

This sponge is an absolute indulgence yet it is low in fat, the only fat coming from the egg yolks. Use this basic fat-free sponge recipe for celebration cakes and puddings with puréed fruit and fat-free fromage frais. They only keep for the day but you'll find that they soon disappear! Although the cake is made with 3 eggs, each serving only contains half an egg at the most. Remember that dietary cholesterol has little effect on blood cholesterol in most people; it is saturated fat which increases blood cholesterol.

summer pudding

Serves 6

1 Cut the crusts off the bread and use to line the base and sides of a 1.2 litre (2 pint) pudding basin, fitting the pieces of bread together closely and trimming to fit. Reserve sufficient bread for the top.

2 Place the fruit, except raspberries and strawberries, in a saucepan with the sugar and water. Heat gently, until the juice begins to run from the fruit and the sugar melts. Remove from the heat, add the liqueur and remaining fruit. Drain the fruit through a nylon sieve, reserving the juice. Spoon the fruit into the lined basin with half the juices and cover with the reserved bread for the top.

3 Press the top with a weighted saucer (cover the weight with clingfilm to prevent tainting the pudding). Stand the basin in a shallow dish to catch any escaping juices and then refrigerate overnight. Cover and refrigerate the remaining juices separately.

4 To serve, remove the weight and run a blunt-edged knife around the pudding. Invert on to an edged dish, shaking gently to release the pudding. Carefully lift off the basin. If the bread looks patchy, brush with the reserved juices. Serve any remaining juices separately. Decorate the pudding with fruit and leaves. Serve with natural yogurt or fromage frais.

300 g (10 oz) stale medium-sliced white bread

875 g (1 ¾ lb) mixed ripe summer fruits, such as redcurrants, whitecurrants, blackcurrants, raspberries, strawberries and cherries, prepared separately

75 g (3 oz) caster sugar

75 ml (3 fl oz) water

a little liqueur, such as framboise, crème de cassis or kirsch

extra fruit and fruit leaves, to decorate

natural yogurt or fromage frais, to serve

NUTRITIONAL FACTS   O Kcals – 215 (903 Kj)   O Fat – 0.7 g, of which 0.2 g saturated   O Sodium – 270 mg

NUTRITIONAL TIPS

This must be everyone's favourite pudding in the summer, when soft fruit is in abundance, and such good news for your healthy heart diet, since it is low in fat. Blackcurrants are not only very high in vitamin C but also one of the highest sources of vitamin E and therefore these small round berries are bursting with great value antioxidant. Every 5 blackcurrants contain 4 mg of vitamin C and 0.02 mg vitamin E.

lemon ricotta cheesecake with blueberries

Preparation time: 30 minutes

Cooking time: about 1 hour

 Serves 10

1 For the crust, mix together the biscuits, sugar, cinnamon and spread in a bowl. In a separate bowl, whisk the egg white until frothy. Stir into the crumb mixture. Press into the bottom of a 23 cm (9 inch) spring form tin. Bake in a preheated oven, 190°C (375°F), Gas Mark 5, for 7–10 minutes until lightly browned. Allow to cool.

2 For the filling, place the ricotta and whole eggs in a food processor or blender and process until smooth. In a bowl, beat together the cheese mixture, sugar, yogurt, lemon juice and rind, flour and vanilla essence until well mixed.

3 In a separate bowl, beat the egg whites until soft peaks form, then fold into the cheese mixture. Spread over the crust. Bake in the oven for 50–55 minutes until the centre is firm to the touch.

4 Run a knife around the edge of the cake to loosen and allow to cool. Remove the sides of the tin, cover the cheesecake and refrigerate for at least 2 hours or up to 1 day. Just before serving, spread the top with fromage frais and cover with blueberries or other fruit.

500 g (1 lb) skimmed ricotta cheese

2 large eggs

75 g (3 oz) sugar

150 g (5 oz) natural yogurt

4 tablespoons lemon juice

grated rind of 2 lemons

2 tablespoons plain flour

2 teaspoons vanilla essence

2 egg whites

150 g (5 oz) natural fromage frais

300 g (10 oz) fresh, frozen and thawed or canned blueberries or other soft fruit

CRUST

125 g (4 oz) plain digestive-type biscuits, crushed

2 tablespoons sugar

1 teaspoon ground cinnamon

15 g (½ oz) unsaturated spread

1 egg white

N U T R I T I O N A L   F A C T S   ◦ Kcals – 177 (744 Kj)   ◦ Fat – 8 g, of which 4 g saturated   ◦ Sodium – 124 mg

N U T R I T I O N A L   T I P S

This cheesecake recipe is low in fat because ricotta cheese is used instead of high-fat cream and cream cheese. There are many low-fat types of ricotta cheese available, read the label and choose the variety with the lowest fat.

The cheesecake crust is also made with very little fat, using egg white to bind rather than the whole egg. Egg white is mainly protein and doesn't contain any fat compared to the yolk which contains 5 g total fat.

mango & pineapple pavlova

1 Whisk the egg whites in a bowl until they are stiff. Fold in 1 tablespoon of the sugar, then gradually whisk in the remainder. The meringue must be glossy and form peaks when spoonfuls are dropped into the bowl. Fold in the black coffee.

2 Spread the meringue mixture over a large sheet of baking paper to form a 20 cm (8 inch) diameter round. Make a slight hollow in the centre of the meringue and cook in a preheated oven, 120°C (250°F), Gas Mark ½, for 1 hour until the meringue is crisp. Remove from the oven and leave to cool on the paper for about 10 minutes before peeling off.

3 When the meringue is cold, fill the hollow in the top with fromage frais. Arrange the mango and pineapple on top, then drizzle the passion fruit seeds and juice over the fruit.

OR YOU COULD TRY...

Try these other combinations of fruit to fill the pavlova:

- Strawberries and mango
- Raspberries and blueberries
- Cherries and nectarines
- Pineapple and papaya

3 egg whites

175 g (6 oz) caster sugar

1 teaspoon strong black coffee

250 g (8 oz) natural fromage frais

125 g (4 oz) mango, diced

125 g (4 oz) fresh pineapple, cut into chunks

1–2 passion fruits

NUTRITIONAL FACTS • Kcals – 245 (1029 Kj) • Fat – less than 1 g, of which negligible saturated • Sodium – 77 mg

NUTRITIONAL TIPS

Pavlova, a much-loved dessert, is surprisingly very low in fat. Meringue is naturally a very low-fat choice since it is made from egg white. You can replace a whole egg with two egg whites in most recipes or use dried egg white powder.

Use fromage frais instead of high fat cream and add any variety of fruit that you like. Orange and yellow fruits, such as mangoes and pineapples, are bursting with ACE antioxidant vitamins.

prune & chocolate crunch

Preparation time: 15 minutes

Cooking time: 30 minutes

(V)

Serves 12

1 Blend the prunes and water in a food processor or blender until almost smooth. Alternatively, mash with a fork.

2 Grease a Swiss-roll type baking tin. Place the prune purée and the remaining ingredients, except those for the topping, in a large bowl and mix well.

3 Spread the mixture evenly in the tin and bake in a preheated oven, 180°C (350°F), Gas Mark 4, for about 30 minutes. Leave to cool in the tin.

4 Before the crunch is completely cold, mix together the ingredients for the topping in a bowl, then spread over the crunch. Cut into 12 squares.

125 g (4 oz) stoned prunes

4 tablespoons water

a little unsaturated spread, for
 greasing

150 g (5 oz) self-raising flour

125 g (4 oz) porridge oats

75 g (3 oz) sugar

3 teaspoons cocoa powder

TOPPING

100 g (3½ oz) icing sugar

2 teaspoons cocoa powder

a little orange juice

NUTRITIONAL FACTS   ○ Kcals – 165 (693 Kj)   ○ Fat – 2 g, of which less than 1 g saturated   ○ Sodium – 75 mg

NUTRITIONAL TIPS
Cocoa is another source of antioxidant polyphenols, similar to those found in fruit, vegetables, red wine and tea, and may have heart-health benefits. Unfortunately they are also very high in fat and sugar.

Puréed prunes are a perfect fat substitute to use in baking. Just substitute the purée for butter or margarine on a direct weight-for-weight measure. Prunes also provide fibre, iron, potassium and vitamin A with no more than a trace of fat, and are contain pectin which helps to create light and fluffy bakes.

pure fruit cake

Preparation time: 15 minutes
Cooking time: 1½ hours

 Makes 12 slices

1 Grease a 1 kg (2 lb) loaf tin. Place the dates in a saucepan with the measured water and heat gently until they are soft. Remove from the heat and mash with a fork until puréed.

2 Place the date purée in a bowl with all the remaining ingredients, except the flaked almonds, and 4 tablespoons of water. Mix together well. Spoon the mixture into the prepared tin and level the top. Sprinkle with flaked almonds.

3 Bake in a preheated oven, 160°C (325°F), Gas Mark 3, for 1½ hours until a skewer inserted into the middle comes out clean. Towards the end of cooking you may need to protect the top of the cake with foil.

4 Allow the cake to cool a little in the tin, then turn out and finish cooling on a wire rack.

a little unsaturated spread, for
  greasing
250 g (8 oz) stoned dates
300 ml (½ pint) water
175 g (6 oz) seedless raisins
125 g (4 oz) sultanas
125 g (4 oz) currants
50 g (2 oz) candied mixed peel,
  chopped
175 g (6 oz) wholemeal plain flour
3 teaspoons baking powder
1 teaspoon mixed spice
grated rind and juice of 1 orange or
  lemon
25 g (1 oz) ground almonds
a few flaked almonds, to decorate

NUTRITIONAL FACTS   ● Kcals – 218 (916 Kj)   ● Fat – 2 g, of which less than 1 g saturated   ● Sodium – 145 mg

NUTRITIONAL TIPS
The puréed dates act as a fat substitute in this recipe and bind all the fruit together to produce a cake that is rich enough for a Christmas cake. Just add almond paste, icing and Santa of course!

banana & raisin tea bread

Preparation time: 10 minutes

Cooking time: 50 minute–1 hour

Serves 12

1 Grease a 1 kg (2 lb) loaf tin. Melt the spread in small saucepan over a low heat. Sift the flours, baking powder and cinnamon into a large bowl. Stir in the sugar, mashed bananas, melted spread, raisins and eggs and beat for 3 minutes until smooth.

2 Turn the mixture into the prepared tin and bake in a preheated oven, 180°C (350°F), Gas Mark 4, for 50 minutes–1 hour until a skewer pierced through the centre comes out clean. Stand the tin on a wire rack to cool slightly before turning out.

3 The tea bread is much tastier if left to mellow for 2–3 days wrapped closely in foil. It can be served thinly sliced and spread with low-fat soft cheese or made into sandwiches with thinly sliced apple or mashed banana.

75 g (3 oz) melted unsaturated spread, plus a little extra for greasing

150 g (5 oz) wholemeal self-raising flour

75 g (3 oz) wholemeal plain flour

1 teaspoon baking powder

1 teaspoon ground cinnamon

75 g (3 oz) brown sugar

3 bananas, well mashed

100 g (3½ oz) seedless raisins

2 eggs, lightly beaten

NUTRITIONAL FACTS ● Kcals – 190 (798 Kj) ● Fat – 7 g, of which 2 g saturated ● Sodium – 110 mg

NUTRITIONAL TIPS
Why go bananas? Latest research shows that a dietary pattern with more servings of fruits, vegetables, grains, nuts and beans than of animal-based foods, low-fat and fat-free dairy produce, and more emphasis on foods that provide potassium, calcium and magnesium help to prevent high blood pressure. All fruit and vegetables are good sources of potassium, but particularly bananas, dried fruit, apricots, rhubarb, blackcurrants, pulses, baked beans, beetroot, sweetcorn, mushrooms, spinach and potatoes.

basic recipes

vegetable stock

Preparation time: 20 minutes
Cooking time: 1 hour 45 minutes
Makes 2.7 litres (4½ pints)

3 medium onions, roughly chopped

5 medium carrots, roughly chopped

3 medium leeks, coarsely sliced

3 medium celery sticks, roughly chopped

3 cabbage leaves, sliced

1 head of lettuce, sliced

6 sprigs of flat leaf parsley with stems, roughly chopped

3 sprigs of thyme

1 bay leaf

3.6 litres (6 pints) cold water

1 Place all the ingredients in a saucepan or stockpot. Cover and bring slowly to the boil. Reduce the heat to a gentle simmer. Skim off any scum. Simmer very gently, covered, for 1 hour, skimming from time to time. Do not disturb or move the stock in any way.

2 Strain well, being careful not to force any of the ingredients through the sieve, since this will cloud the stock. Allow to cool, then cover and refrigerate.

○ fat-free

○ Sodium – 90 mg

chicken stock

Preparation time: 10 minutes
Cooking time: 2–3 hours, plus chilling
Makes 2.5 litres (4 pints)

1.5 kg (3 lb) fresh chicken

1 onion, stuck with three cloves

2 carrots, coarsely sliced

2 celery sticks, coarsely sliced

1 head of garlic, cloves separated and unpeeled

6 sprigs of flat leaf parsley with stems

3 sprigs of fresh thyme

1 bay leaf

2.75 litres (5 pints) cold water, to cover by at least 7 cm (3 inches)

1 Place all the ingredients in a large saucepan or stockpot. Cover and bring slowly to the boil. Reduce the heat to a gentle simmer. Skim off any scum. Simmer very gently, partially covered, for 2–3 hours for a rich stock, skimming from time to time. Do not disturb or move the stock in any way.

2 Strain well, being careful not to force any of the ingredients through the sieve, as this will cloud the stock. Allow to cool, then cover and refrigerate for several hours before removing all the solidified fat.

○ fat-free

○ Sodium – 94 mg

olive vinaigrette

Preparation time: 5 minutes
Makes 300 ml (½ pint)

125 ml (4 fl oz) balsamic vinegar

125 ml (4 fl oz) lime juice

2 garlic cloves, crushed

3 black olives, pitted

1 tablespoon Dijon mustard

pinch of sugar

1 Place all the ingredients in a screw-top jar, replace the lid and shake well. Store in the refrigerator for up to 1 week.

- Kcals – 82 (344 Kj)
- Fat – 3 g, of which less than 1 g saturated
- Sodium – 800 mg

ginger & garlic paste

Preparation time: 5 minutes
Makes 250 g (8 oz)

125 g (4 oz) fresh root ginger, peeled and cut into chunks

125 g (4 oz) peeled garlic cloves

1 Process the ginger with the garlic cloves in a food processor or blender with a very little water, just to aid processing. Spoon into an airtight screw-top jar and store in the refrigerator for up to 3 weeks. Alternatively, place small quantities in a specially reserved ice-cube tray. Or spread the paste on to a baking sheet, freeze, then remove the slab and break into pieces. Store in a plastic freezer bag.

- Kcals – 184 (773 Kj)
- Fat – 2 g, of which less than 1 g saturated
- Sodium – 19 mg

fruity dressing

Preparation time: a few minutes
Makes 100 ml (3½ oz)

2 teaspoons wholegrain mustard

4 tablespoons balsamic vinegar

1 tablespoon olive oil

1 tablespoon orange or apple juice

freshly ground black pepper

1 Place the wholegrain mustard, balsamic vinegar, olive oil, orange or apple juice and pepper in a screw-top jar, replace the lid and shake well to combine. Store in the refrigerator for up to 7 days.

- Kcals – 130 (340 Kj)
- Fat – 12g, of which less than 2 g saturated
- Sodium – 166 mg

*The nutritional facts for all recipes in this section are for the whole recipe quantity.

teriyaki sauce

Preparation time: a few minutes
Cooking time: a few minutes
Makes 100 ml (3½ oz)

1 shallot, finely sliced

1 teaspoon minced fresh root ginger

50 ml (2 fl oz) rice wine vinegar or sherry

2 tablespoons reduced-salt soy sauce

1 teaspoon honey

2 tablespoons lime or lemon juice

1 teaspoon sesame oil

1 Place the shallot, ginger, vinegar or sherry, soy sauce, honey and 1 tablespoon lime or lemon juice in a small saucepan over medium heat. Stir in the sesame oil and remaining lime juice and heat through.

- Kcals – 140 (588 Kj)
- Fat – 3 g, of which less than 1 g saturated
- Sodium – 10 mg

herbed yogurt & cucumber sauce

Preparation time: 5 minutes, plus chilling
Makes 2–3 servings

125 g (4 oz) grated cucumber

1 tablespoon chopped dill or mint

200 g (7 oz) natural yogurt

1 tablespoon lime or lemon juice

freshly ground black pepper

1 Mix the ingredients together, cover and chill in the refrigerator for about 30 minutes before serving to allow the flavours to develop.

- Kcals – 125 (525 Kj)
- Fat – 2g, of which less than 1 g saturated
- Sodium – 170 mg

tomato salsa

Preparation time: 10 minutes, plus infusing
Makes 8 servings

500 g (1 lb) ripe tomatoes, skinned and deseeded

1 small onion, finely chopped

1–3 green chillies, deseeded and finely chopped

1 tablespoon white vinegar

pinch of sugar

2 tablespoons chopped fresh coriander or parsley

freshly ground black pepper

1 Finely chop the tomatoes by hand or process very briefly in a food processor or blender. Mix with the remaining ingredients. Leave for 30 minutes for the flavours to infuse. The salsa will keep for up to a week in the refrigerator.

- Kcals – 115 (483 Kj)
- Fat – 2 g, of which less than 1 g saturated
- Sodium – 50 mg

mango salsa

Preparation time: 10 minutes, plus infusing
Makes 6 servings

1 mango

200 g (7 oz) ripe tomatoes, skinned, deseeded and chopped

1 green chilli, deseeded and finely chopped

1 tablespoon chopped mint

1 tablespoon chopped fresh coriander

juice of 1 lime

1 tablespoon olive oil

pinch of sugar

freshly ground black pepper

1 For the salsa, cut the mango lengthways either side of the thin central stone. Cut away the skin from the flesh. Finely chop the flesh and place in a bowl with the tomatoes.

2 Add the remaining salsa ingredients. Cover and refrigerate for at least 30 minutes to allow the flavours to infuse. (The salsa will keep for up to 1 week in the refrigerator.)

- Kcals – 266 (1114 Kj)
- Fat – 13.4g of fat of which 1.8g is saturated fat
- Sodium – trace

index

acknowledgements

Thank you to all at the Family Heart Association, especially Michael Livingston for giving me time to write this book and Gill Stokes who gave me some of her family's favourite recipes. To all at The Conquest Hospital, Hastings, my friends and colleagues in The Nutrition and Dietetic Department for their departmental recipes and to Alison Hassell, Senior Dietitian for working with me on 'Making Changes'. To all in Cardiology, especially Dr Richard Wray, Cardiologist for his constant support and encouragement, the Cardiac Rehabilitation Team and all my patients over the years whom I have been privileged to meet and who have taught me so much. To my own dear children, Lottie, Sam and Tom, for their resilience – it can't be easy having such a 'passionate' dietitian for a Mum! Finally, to Jonathan for his love, hours of patience and help with this book.

THE AUTHOR
Jacqui Lynas (BSc SRD) is a state-registered dietician with a specialist interest in heart-disease prevention. She works for the Family Heart Association and is an acknowledged expert in her field with over 20 years' experience. She is a regular contributor to medical textbooks, journals and magazines, as well as being a popular speaker at scientific meetings.

Photographic Acknowledgements in Source Order

Getty Images/Image Bank 7 top right, 16 Top, 25 bottom, /Stone 7 bottom, 9, 13, 16 bottom.
Octopus Publishing Group Limited/David Jordan 27 detail 1, 29 bottom right/Sandra Lane 28 top left, /William Lingwood 26 detail 1, detail 2, 28 top centre left, 29 top centre right, /Sean Myers 28 bottom centre left, /William Reavell 3, 7 top left, 11, 17 top, 17 bottom, 18, 20 top, 20 bottom, 21 top, 21 bottom, 23, 24, 25 right, 26 detail 3, 26 detail 4, 26 detail 5, 26 detail 6, 27 detail 2, 27 detail 3, 27 detail 4, 27 detail 6, 27 detail 7, 28 bottom left, 29 top left, 29 top right, 29 bottom left, 29 bottom centre left, 29 bottom centre right, 32 top left, 32 centre left, 32 centre right, 32 top right, 32 bottom right, 32 bottom left, 33 top left, 33 centre left, 33 top right, 33 centre right, 33 bottom right, 33 bottom left, 35 top left, 35 top right, 35 Bottom, 36 top centre, 36 top right, 37, 39, 43, 44 top centre, 44 top right, 47, 51, 55, 56 top centre, 56 top right, 59, 63, 67, 70 top centre, 70 top right, 71, 75, 79, 83, 86 top centre, 86 top right, 87, 91, 93, 97, 99, 102 top centre, 102 top right, 103, 107, 111, 115, 116 top centre, 116 top right, 119, 123, 124 top centre, 124 top right, 127, 131, 133, 137, /Simon Smith 27 detail 5, 28 bottom centre right, /Ian Wallace 28 bottom right, 29 top centre left, /Philip Webb 28 top right, 28 top centre right.
Science Photo Library 10 top, 10 bottom.

Executive Editor **Nicky Hill**
Editor **Abi Rowsell**
Senior Designer **Joanna Bennett**
Designer **Claire Harvey**
Photographer **William Reavell**
Home Economist **Louise Blair**
Picture Researcher **Zoë Holterman**
Production Controller **Viv Cracknell**